6 WEEK FINALS

The Complete System for Audition Success

Sharon Sparrow

Assistant Principal Flute

Detroit Symphony Orchestra

THEODORE PRESSER COMPANY

CONTENTS

Testimonials 3
Foreword 4
Introduction 6
A Choice 7
Conditioning 7
SIX WEEKS AND COUNTING 10
Week 6 10
Week 5 19
Week 4 26
Week 3 33
Week 2 39
Week 1 45
Audition Day! 49
The Aftermath: Life After Audition Day 60
Acknowledgments 64
Permissions 64

© 2016 by Theodore Presser Company
All Rights Reserved
Printed in U.S.A.
International Copyright Secured

Unauthorized copying, arranging, adapting, recording, or digital storage or transmission is an infringement of copyright. Infringers are liable under the law.

"Words can't express how thankful I am to have used Sharon Sparrow's book, 6 Weeks to Finals, which resulted in me winning the 2nd Flute position with the Detroit Symphony Orchestra. This method helped me to feel more confident than ever, knowing that I had prepared in every conceivable way. Sharon's triathlon approach guides the reader through meticulous practice routines, numerous mock auditions, and the often undervalued component of mental training. The latter component especially helped me to overcome an emotional attachment to the job, resulting in three rounds of auditions, a trial week, and a job offer with the DSO. I cannot praise Sharon's book enough!"

—*Amanda Blaikie*
2nd Flute, Detroit Symphony Orchestra

"Auditions present so many challenges and hurdles to conquer that preparing in a really organized and methodical manner is the only way to approach them and hope for a successful outcome. Sharon Sparrow's six-week method for audition preparation is such an amazing tool to add to anyone's routine. Offering solutions to everything from excerpt organization to the scheduling of mock auditions, it helps put you in the correct mindset for the various stages of the process, which is a vital part of being as successful as possible on the day of the audition itself. I believe that using Sharon's process was essential and pushed me in the right direction in the preparation of the first orchestral audition that I won, and I would do the same for any future auditions!"

— *Zachariah Galatis*
Solo Piccolo, Oregon Symphony

6 Weeks to Finals is a must-read for anyone taking professional auditions. Sharon Sparrow's insight to the process opened a whole new approach for me. Using her techniques, I quickly won a regional orchestra position. Fast forward three months, and I went from prelim to extended final rounds, to 2-week trial, to winning a year-long contract with the San Francisco Symphony! I could not have achieved my current successes without her advice.

— *Steve Sanchez*
Clarinet, Monterey Symphony
Extra Clarinet, San Francisco Symphony

"Sitting on countless audition committees in the past 25 years, only two performances stand out in my memory as being nearly flawless. Each excerpt was executed note perfectly with musical intention in every note and phrase. As each excerpt passed, my mental checklist of what I was listening for was completely satisfied, which is rare! I came to find out later that both performers used the 6 Weeks to Finals preparation method, one of whom was Ms. Sparrow herself at her first successful audition here in Detroit!"

-*Jeffery Zook*
Piccolo, Detroit Symphony Orchestra

FOREWORD
by Jeffrey Barker, Associate Principal Flute, Seattle Symphony

A few months ago, I reached a life-long goal, landing a dream job playing in the Seattle Symphony, my hometown orchestra. This wonderful outcome came at the end of a strenuous and challenging process, including a four-day long audition and trial week rehearsing and performing with the orchestra. The path that led me here was, of course, much more complicated, involving many years of hard work, invaluable guidance from teachers and mentors, countless failures and frustrations, and a long, personal evolution in my mindset and strategy for auditions.

When I first began taking orchestral auditions, I had a negative outlook on the challenge before me, one that was shared and reinforced by many other aspiring orchestral musicians I knew. We viewed auditions as a necessary evil, a flawed process that's costly and demoralizing to the participants and that often fails to result in hiring the best candidate for the position. I gradually learned that this way of thinking was depressing and counterproductive. Before I was able to find any success in auditions, I had to change my outlook. I began to see auditions as a chance to tap into enormous sources of motivation and inspiration, an opportunity to achieve a higher level of musicianship than would otherwise be possible. I started to realize that despite all the frustrating and flawed parts, much of my success or failure in an audition was still under my direct control, and that I owed it to myself to focus all my energy on preparing myself to perform well. Perhaps most important, I began to understand how vital it was to have a clear and effective plan that I could follow in the weeks leading up to an audition, in order to feel confident that I was putting myself in the best possible position to succeed.

The plan that raised me to a higher level of competitiveness and changed the way I think and feel about auditions is Sharon Sparrow's 6 WEEKS TO FINALS. I first encountered Sharon's plan in a condensed form, through an e-mail circulating among musicians on the audition circuit. It was a brief summary of Sharon's method that described the basic philosophy of the plan. Around the time a friend shared this e-mail with me, I got to know Sharon personally when I began subbing with the Detroit Symphony. There was a principal flute audition for a very good orchestra coming up soon that I badly wanted to win. Sharon was kind enough to coach me through my preparation, and she gave me much more detail on her six-week plan. I decided to follow her plan 100%, to dive right into it wholeheartedly and see what happened.

Preparing for this audition was exhilarating and transformative. I found that Sharon's method organized my time in such a productive and efficient way that I never doubted I was making great progress toward my goal. The plan required me to be completely honest with myself about all the weaknesses in my playing and the flaws in my excerpts, which wasn't always easy. But after six weeks of thorough, diligent work, I could feel I was much better prepared than I'd ever been before. I was mentally focused and felt confident I would be able to walk on stage and play the way I intended. The anxiety and restlessness I normally felt in the days leading up to an audition were replaced with excited anticipation. I couldn't wait to go play this audition.

I didn't end up winning the job, but after a few days of being sad about that, I quickly recognized this audition as a success. The hard work I had done in my preparation had paid off in tangible ways throughout the process. I walked into each round with an unfamiliar feeling of confidence and freedom, rather than struggling through mental battles like I often had in past auditions. And my preparation proved itself in the results, too. Over the course of two days, I advanced through the preliminary, semifinal, and final round, all the way to a super-final round with just me and one other candidate. I wasn't perfect in any of these rounds, but I was proud of how I played in each of them, even in the super-final round that I didn't win. I knew I had accurately represented who I was as a musician, and I had great confidence that I would be able to replicate this type of preparation and performance in future auditions.

I have followed Sharon's plan diligently for all the auditions I've done since, including my recent successful one in Seattle. I know of many other musicians who have found similar success with this plan. If you are motivated to succeed in auditions but find that you consistently underperform your potential, following 6 WEEKS TO FINALS for your next audition is very likely to have a huge impact. The tremendous motivation and discipline required to win an audition comes from within, but the plan laid out in this book will channel your efforts into outstanding results better than any other method I've seen.

Jeffrey Barker with the Seattle Symphony   *photo credit: Brandon Patoc*

INTRODUCTION by Sharon Sparrow

I took my very first orchestral audition one month after I graduated from Juilliard, having little clue of the arena I was about to enter for the next 25 years! Since that first audition, which I did not win, I've taken countless auditions, studying the art of achieving success at them along the way. I landed my first job as Principal Flute in the Memphis Symphony on a one-year position, and after that year won a permanent position as Principal Flute in the Fort Wayne Philharmonic. I continued taking auditions regularly, always trying for that "bigger" job, usually getting close but never winning the position.

Meanwhile, life continued and I married the Principal Clarinet of my orchestra and started a family. Just after finishing my ninth season in Fort Wayne, my life took a sudden twist as I contracted a severe case of encephalitis (inflammation of the brain) resulting from chicken pox. I lost almost all motor function and the ability to form words and sentences for many months. But luckily, the virus slowly began to reverse itself, and little by little, I regained all my facility.

It was at this time the audition for 2nd Flute in the Detroit Symphony was announced, and I saw that audition as a perfect opportunity to test my resilience and ability to take an audition again. At the time I had a 3-year-old and a 1-year-old at home, so time management was of the essence. It was in these two months before the Detroit audition that my initial "6-Week Plan" was conceived.

Always being a very organized person, I wanted to design a practice method that I could follow and stick to during these very important weeks. I needed a detailed plan to stay on task and not be distracted by my daily duties and along with the illness that was thankfully getting better each day. I approached this audition quite differently from the many I had taken before, replacing my usual outcome goals with some basic performance goals, spending much more time exploring the mental aspect of auditioning as well as just practicing the flute. This new strategy along with the detailed, methodical, and thorough preparation plan I had devised and stuck to ultimately won me the 2nd Flute position at that audition in Detroit!

I jotted down notes from this plan, and eventually came up with a specific outline which I presented at the National Flute Association Convention in NYC in 2009. It became very clear to me that I was not alone, and that many flutists struggled with finding an organized method to prepare for orchestral auditions. Following this NFA presentation, I began getting many calls and requests to share my plan, and was beyond thrilled when people I was coaching began reaching the finals and even winning some of the open positions! By this point I had not only taken more auditions, having a great deal of success at each one, but had also been able to serve on many orchestral audition committees. I had so much new information to add to my original outline, and I felt ready and eager to help the many people taking auditions with my plan for organizing their time and practice routines leading up to the audition day.

By sharing my experiments and insights to this very specific task of auditioning, I've had the great pleasure to watch many who were struggling with auditions finally break out of preliminary rounds and even more importantly gain immense confidence through the discipline and structure it provides. I know that when approached with great discipline, these pages will provide you with a new set of tools and extra confidence to achieve success on a whole new level at your next audition!

I strongly recommend that you read this book from beginning to end, jotting down some notes along the way, and then return to SIX WEEKS AND COUNTING (page 10) to begin your training.

A CHOICE

I love college basketball. Growing up in Syracuse, NY, it was difficult not to be swept up in the energy, madness, and pure enjoyment of the college basketball season year after year. The excitement was intoxicating, and the passion of the coaches and teams was pure inspiration. This is why a few months before one of the most important auditions I'd ever take, I stumbled across a life changing book written by University of Kentucky (now University of Louisville) basketball coach Rick Pitino entitled "*Success is a Choice.*" I'd always been fascinated by Coach Pitino, and even something about the title of his new book intrigued me.

Choosing success was something I'd never really thought about. It inspired me to re-evaluate the whole idea of taking auditions. Honestly, *auditions are a choice*. No one ever forced me to take an audition. Auditions were a means to an end that I knew I wanted, so more often than not, I made the *choice* to take audition after audition. It was a very freeing thought, knowing that everything I would need to do in the ensuing weeks until audition day was purely and entirely *my choice*.

After committing to this choice, I decided to study Pitino's book to learn that since I had made the choice to audition, I needed to shift my thinking and also make the choice to succeed!

So as you begin this book and commit to the many steps, countless hours of practice, breaking new records of personal growth, remember that this is *your* choice. And now you will be presented with the many tools you will need to turn your choice into success!

CONDITIONING

I've spent countless hours watching Grand Slam tennis tournaments. Pete Sampras, Andre Agassi, Serena Williams, Rafael Nadal, and Roger Federer, just to name a few, have spent many hours flashing across my TV screen in hundreds of matches and tournaments. I'm in awe of their focus, stamina, athleticism, passion, drive, and power. It's as if by just watching them, I could absorb some of their mojo into my flute playing purely by osmosis!

I took my last audition right after the 2015 French Open, having again spent many hours watching the tournament. When I didn't advance to the final round, I really began to question myself, as I thought I'd developed a tried and true method for taking auditions. However, I felt I could not possibly validate this method anymore, as I hadn't reached the final round of this audition.

Thinking back to the tennis matches I'd just watched, suddenly a light bulb went on! I had prepared for the "match" itself, but skipped the all important steps that should have come even BEFORE the 6-week plan began... *conditioning!* Even freshman football players in high school know about this; they spend two weeks in "conditioning" camp before actual football practices even begin. Conditioning for tennis players involves weight training, running, muscle strengthening, hand-eye coordination drills, and sprints, and every new tournament begins with several weeks in the gym for them far in advance of tournament date, before even stepping foot on the court or hitting a tennis ball.

Conditioning for flute players involves scales, arpeggios, double-tonguing exercises, triple-tonguing exercises, scores of difficult etudes, long tones, breath control exercises, diminuendos and releases with the tuner just to name a few. I was lulled into the false belief that because I play a high-level job every day, have little problem executing anything on my stand, and am on the stage day after day, that my audition preparation could begin directly with the excerpts. *Lesson Learned!* Imagine if my tennis idols thought and prepared this way, skipping all of the conditioning before ever setting foot on the court for their practice? I doubt they would be the ones reaching the finals year after year!

Think about it – the excerpts that are placed on audition lists are likely the most difficult, most technical snippets we'll ever play in the chair. And in auditions, there is very little margin for error. I believe college students have a slight advantage here, as they are afforded the time and encouragement to follow a weekly conditioning routine, sometimes even guided by their teachers. Looking back over the last 6 months before this audition, I admit, although almost embarrassingly, that I could not even remember the last time I played through an entire etude or spent more than 15 minutes repeating my Taffanel/Gaubert, Maquarre, or Reichert. I relied daily only on my "conditioning bank," the one I built up in college, grad school, and the ensuing years post-grad in the private studio of the technical master Geoffrey Gilbert.

I had convinced myself I didn't have time for new conditioning, with all the notes in the many folders, and pieces on my practice stand, week after week needed for the job I was being paid to play. *I couldn't have been more wrong!* Just like athletes, when you choose to enter the competition or audition ring, you must be in the best shape of your life for that moment! You *must* take the time to rebuild, re-hone your basic foundation and skills, no matter how solid you think or believe they may be. You must be able to master the flute with complete ease, having retrained and solidified all your muscle memory. This can take anywhere from a few weeks to many months before you hit the audition stage or begin the 6 Weeks to Finals training plan, so it's best to start conditioning TODAY, whether an audition is in your near future or not!

(Opening of Andersen Etude Op. 60, No. 3)

MENTAL CONDITIONING

A large part of the 6-week plan involves the extremely important, yet often overlooked, element of mental preparation. You can begin to "condition" for this as well as you condition your fingers. If you are already seasoned in the art of meditation, you may want to begin incorporating this to your daily regimen with the tools you already have. If you are a novice at this, I can share a couple of things that I use to get started and have found extremely helpful.

Each day I set aside anywhere from 6 to 15 minutes for what I call "positive meditation." This is a time where I am alone and in a quiet space so I can shut out all the outside disturbances and voices, and listen to my inner voice in a calm and relaxed state. I use both meditative music and a timer for this. For music, I love the tracks of the CD titled "Dreamland" by the wonderful Canadian flutist Laura Nashman. This and other meditation CDs are available on the *spa-la-la.com* website. For me, meditation begins with breathing, so once the music begins playing I take many full and relaxing breaths, inhaling and exhaling very slowly. Next I begin to incorporate my list of positive suggestions, taking time to breathe with every suggestion I feed myself. Everyone's positive suggestions will and should be different and very personal. But you may need some audition-specific ones to get you started in your conditioning regime. Try the following, or any variations of these that resonate with you:

"I am worthy, I am strong."
"I am capable of working very hard toward my goals."
"I look forward to the challenge of becoming the best player I can possibly be."
"I am grateful for this challenge and all that it entails."

These, of course, are just suggestions and are meant to stimulate your own creative positive thoughts for your endeavor. Once in place, set your timer for anywhere from 6 to 15 minutes, and begin to incorporate this into your daily regimen. Not only will it begin to have an effect on how you feel every single day, but it will be conditioning you for the more intense mental training and visualization exercises explained later that you will incorporate into your 6-week program for a successful audition!

Once you are "conditioned," you're ready to begin the 6-week training that will lead you to the final round!

Six Weeks and Counting

WEEK 6

EQUIPMENT

YOUR FLUTES: Your audition is six weeks away, so now's the time to make sure your equipment is assembled and that your instruments are in the best shape possible. Hopefully you have not been putting off that overhaul, as your flute will log a ton of mileage in these next six weeks, and you must be confident that it's up to the task. If you notice ANY leaks, worn or torn pads, mechanism sluggishness, or it's just plain dirty, take the time *right now* to get it in the best working condition possible in the least amount of time. I am definitely guilty of putting off scheduled maintenance and ignoring little glitches, but when it comes down to it, you have the Indy 500 only six weeks away, so you want your car to be able to perform at its highest level!

If you have put off or are in need of a COA (clean, oil, adjust), 10 weeks out is an ideal time. At 8 weeks you will need to engage in some pretty hefty "conditioning," and once the 6-week plan begins you won't want to be without your flute for a minute!

TUNER: I am a huge fan of any Korg chromatic tuner which registers pitch with a moving needle, and where the fixed pitch is adjustable (A=440, or 441, etc). Many musicians have tuner apps on their phones, but there are two reasons I don't recommend this while doing audition prep work.

1)Some phone tuner apps have trouble deciphering the high partials of the flute sound, and register incorrectly. Recently a student was playing one note, while the app tuner registered a totally different pitch.

2) In all honesty, phones are distracting. Even if you are "only" using it for the tuning app, there may be the possibility of it distracting you with calls, texts, etc. I have found I do my most focused practicing when my phone is not in the room with me. Tuning is such an important part of your preparation, so please take this suggestion while picking out a tuner for your 6-week program.

METRONOME: For some of the exercises in this book, the best choice of a metronome is one with a dial. I have not had the same success with phone app metronomes, the "meeping" metronomes, or the ones that you increase digitally and decrease digitally one number at a time. I've personally found the most helpful metronome to be the Wittner MT-50, or any similar metronome. They are simple, loud, can easily be changed with the dial, readily available at local instrument stores, and extremely inexpensive.

RECORDING DEVICE: I've been happy for many years using the Garage Band app on my Macbook. I can't tell you how many students I've asked to record themselves who tell me they do NOT own any recording device. I then ask if they have a smartphone, tablet, or computer of any kind, because they all have microphones (or input jacks) and all have recording apps. They always say yes, but most didn't realize how useful Garage Band or other apps can be, or even that they already have recording apps handy. There are many tutorials on YouTube that explain how to use these very useful tools. Even the "voice memo" on most phones will be acceptable for practice, although upgrading a bit from that could definitely not hurt. Many students prefer pocket-size digital recorders. It does not need to be recording studio quality, but it is most useful if you can evaluate your true sound, and especially different levels of sound, ranging from pianissimo to fortissimo in all registers!

BLANK STAFF PAPER: You may want to use staff paper to design your own personal warm-up for a specific audition, as explained later in the "Useful Warm-up" section.

INDEX CARDS: That's right! Your average pack of drug store blank index cards. Believe it or not, these are *just as important* as all other things on this equipment list!

PORTABLE LISTENING DEVICE: One of your first tasks in Week 6 is to make a playlist of all of the excerpts on the audition list. It will be useful to listen to many recordings of each excerpt, as tempos will vary significantly with each conductor. If the orchestra you're auditioning for has a recording with the current conductor, *use that one*!

With so many internet streaming options now available, it's much easier to find multiple recordings than it was even a few years ago. One of the best resources that we often forget about is the local library. Even in my current small town of Grosse Pointe, Michigan, there's an overwhelming abundance of amazing classical CDs available there to listen to, and for *free*! Be careful not to rely entirely on YouTube, as there are many recordings there that you should NOT be getting ideas from, as they are pretty misleading as far as tempo and quality of performance. One tip that I tell students who ask what is an "appropriate" tempo for a particular excerpt is to listen to five different recordings of the excerpt, making a note of each tempo (using your metronome) and then take the exact average of the tempos. Believe it or not, this always works!

If this is your first time doing so, do not become discouraged with the amount of time making this playlist takes. Keep in mind that many flute audition lists are very similar, so after you make this one, each new one will only take a few more minutes to update!

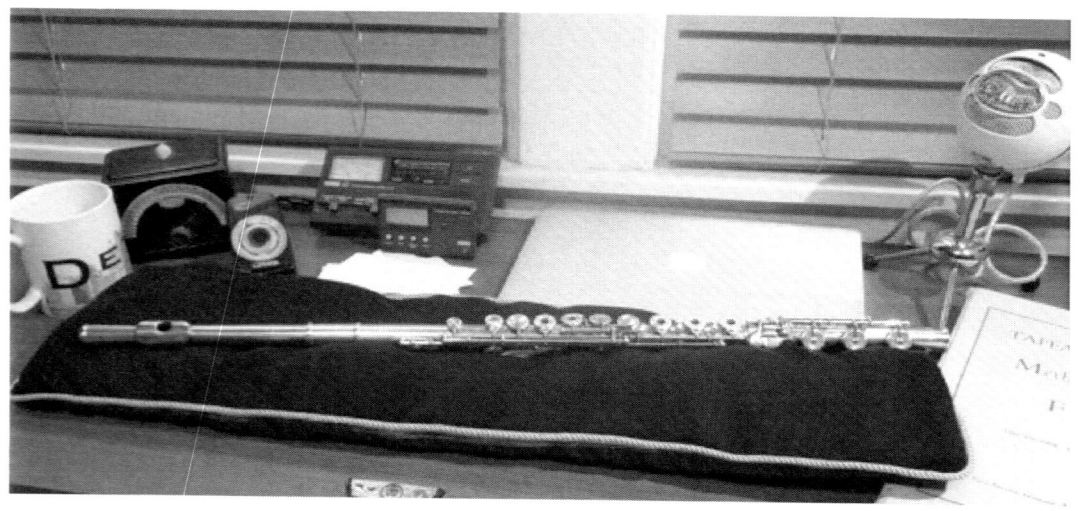

My "equipment" table all ready to begin Week 6!

AUDITION LISTS: These are typically accessible on the orchestra's website up to 2 months before an audition. Your task at the beginning of this week is to assemble every excerpt on the upcoming audition. Get each excerpt organized so you can travel to your nearest office-supply store to make your necessary Audition Booklet! Every single note that you might play at the audition (except sightreading, of course) needs to be in this Audition Booklet!

If the orchestra lists "entire piece," as sometimes is the case with Ravel's *Daphnis et Chloe*, or Prokofiev's *Classical Symphony* to name a couple, then you must have the entire part for these in your booklet! Don't cut corners! I've heard many audition horror stories where the candidate either forgot or ignored a tutti section that was on the list, and never practiced that section thinking it wasn't important and would never be asked. I confess, this happened to me once as well many, many years ago… I was in the final round for a job that I really wanted. *Daphnis (entire piece)* was on the list. I prepared the solo, the opening, the ensuing noodles, and the treacherous part at the end that begins at m.214. However, I always stopped my practice at m.221. I never thought any committee would be interested in that little part filling in m.221 to the end of the piece, so I never even played through it. At this point in my career, I hadn't yet performed *Daphnis*. At this audition, I was thrilled to have advanced through the preliminary and semi-final rounds. In the finals, however, one part near the very end of the round was marked to play "*m.214 to END OF PIECE.*" Uh oh! I confidently and accurately strode through measures 214-221 like a champ, then when I hit those triplets, started fumbling like a football player running with the ball toward the goal line on the 5 yard line who suddenly had butter all over his hands! By the third measure in I'd become completely derailed and couldn't go on. There was silence from the committee, probably a bit of disbelief! After what seemed like an eternity, a voice said "Could the candidate please repeat m.214 to the end?" Whew! A second chance! Again, sailed through like a champ, and again, fumbled equally badly when hitting the triplets! This time it was like someone running gracefully then hitting an unexpected patch of ice! And again, I could not even get to the end! Once again, total silence for what seemed like forever. Then a very disappointed voice said "thank you." Needless to say, I did not get that job. And I also did not ever again ignore one single note of music that was on an audition list!!

Ravel: Daphnis et Chloe

Now that you've assembled all your excerpts in their entirety, make a booklet in alphabetical order, spiral bound. I usually use a print-out of the list as my cover page. Be sure to check that page turns are correct, as you don't want to be practicing an excerpt out of your booklet and have to stop and turn a page! Since making multiple booklets at the same time is just as easy as making one, I always make three booklets, as you'll want your "mock committee(s)" to have a booklet to look at during your mock auditions so they can really help with useful comments. *This takes time*! But, please trust me, the time you'll save over the next 6 weeks, once you have this booklet to practice from, will be worth the effort it took to make it, 20 times over!

"I RESPECTFULLY DECLINE"

When I was playing in the Fort Wayne Philharmonic, there were always many more committee spots to fill than musicians who wanted to be on these committees. I imagine this is the case with most orchestras. Each year there would be an orchestra meeting where nominations were taken for spots on these committees. More often than not, we would hear our name at this meeting suddenly being nominated for a committee we had no intention of being on. It was at these meetings that I learned the ever popular phrase *"I respectfully decline."* It was perfect! It was respectful. It needed no explanation. There was no further ensuing discussion. No one was ever offended by this polite refusal to be nominated. So I advise you to practice this phrase out loud over and over, because as you begin these six weeks of training, you must clear as much time as possible in your schedule and not be afraid to "respectfully decline" ANYTHING that will take your focus or time away from your upcoming audition. Anything you can reasonably decline, do so! Keep in mind, this is a very short period of time with a definite end date, and a significant goal to be acquired. If you can afford to turn down extra gigs, extra students, committee work, and vacations during this time, remind yourself that achieving success at the audition will make up tenfold for everything you passed on or put on hold for these 6 weeks.

IT'S A TRIATHLON, NOT A MARATHON

One of the biggest mistakes I see students making in preparing for orchestral auditions is that they only simply practice. They practice and practice and practice the excerpts on the list diligently, take the audition, and come away mystified when they don't advance past the preliminary round. "I practiced SO much, I don't understand!" This is why I promote the theory that audition taking is NOT a marathon, where one focuses training solely on running, but a triathlon, where equal focus must be given to running, swimming, AND biking. The running is our Practicing. We are all trained in that, and to many of us, that part comes naturally. We have learned to spend many hours at practicing from an early age, and we feel comfortable doing it. Tell us to get to the practice room, we say "great"! That is basically our home away from home and has been for many years. But now you must add some swimming to the mix! Swimming for the auditionee is MENTAL TRAINING. Auditions are a unique experience and training your head for those brief minutes on stage is equally important to training your fingers to execute the notes on the page.

The legendary tennis player Chris Evert once wrote in *Tennis Magazine*,
> "One aspect that's tougher to train is the mental part of the game. You can measure physical gains, but the mind is intangible. It's much harder to teach players how to become fitter between the ears than it is to clean up their diets."[1]

This is true of musicians as well. However, there are several resources available to you if you just know where and how to look for them. I've studied many excellent mental toughness training books, primarily geared toward athletes, but equally adaptable to musicians. Substitute a few words here and there, and you have yourself a perfect mental training book for auditions! The books that have resonated the most with me are:

> *The Mental Game* by James Loehr
> *Mental Toughness Training for Sports* by James Loehr
> *The Inner Game of Tennis* by W. Timothy Gallwey
> *Success Is a Choice* by Rick Pitino
> *Pressure Is a Privilege* by Billie Jean King
> *The Inner Game of Music* by Barry Green
> *A Soprano on Her Head* by Eloise Ristad
> *Effortless Mastery* by Kenny Werner
> *Performance Success* by Don Greene
> *Wooden: A Lifetime of Observations and Reflections On and Off the Court*
>   by John Wooden with Steve Jamison

Don Greene also has a great website *(dongreene.com)* where you can download his books and useful training videos as well. Outside of the music and sports arenas, there are additional resources available, such as Source Movement, comprised of two former orchestral musicians, now High Performance coaches, who creatively guide each individual person to overcome their fears and reach their own "full potential self" in any situation, especially auditions. They're achieving lots of success working with musicians, and they can be found at *sourcemovement.com/peakperformance*. This mental toughness part of the triathlon I believe gets the least amount of attention, but is maybe the most important part of the three to achieve success. So it's time to head online to research and purchase at the very least one of these books or resources to use as a tool for this all important piece of the audition triathlon.

The third equal part of audition preparation lies in the mock audition. The 5-20 minutes you spend on stage executing excerpts in random order one after another to a huge hall that is completely silent is not at all like practicing. This is a learned art in itself, and it must take an equal role in your preparation. From daily random mock auditions for your recording device to scheduled formal mocks with an assembled committee of one to four listeners, this crucial part of your triathlon cannot be diminished or ignored.

This 6-week program will walk you through all the important steps in all three areas you'll need to strengthen to succeed at this triathlon:

Practicing — Mental training — Mock auditions.

Let's begin!

DEVELOPING A "USEFUL WARM-UP"

I'm a firm believer in warm-ups. I begin practice every single day with what I call a "useful warm-up." Playing long tones daily are crucial to solidifying your basic foundation, and when could you possibly need a stronger foundation than when you prepare for an audition?

There are scores and scores of warm up books available, as well as warm-up routines that have been taught and coached to you from numerous teachers, peers, and mentors. At this moment, though, you want to be able to merge all those books, all of the warm up advice, and add in your own common sense to develop the most useful warm up designed specifically for *your* weaknesses for the audition you are about to take.

This is where blank staff paper comes into play. Think about each excerpt, and then develop a warm up that tackles the difficult parts of it. For example, I'll use the Beethoven *Leonore Overture No. 3* opening. The high G *ff* entrance followed by the immediate ⟩ *p*, then the ensuing scale down in *p*, ending on a *pp* F♯ is a definite challenge, and very rarely played stunningly in an audition.

How about turning that into a warm-up long-tone exercise? How about just using the fortissimo G with a measured count diminuendo to *pp*? How about then transposing that up a half step to A♭? Then up another half-step to A, and so on to high C? I like to start on a *ff* high G, watching both the second hand of the clock and my tuner. (A digital clock works fine but is just not as much fun to watch.) Take 5 seconds to diminuendo to *p*, and then hold that note at a *p* dynamic for 30 seconds, diminuendo to *pp*, then release. I repeat this several times, sometimes going up in half steps, sometimes going down. That's a small piece of a useful warm up for this audition!

Looking ahead, there are the B Major triplets also in *pp*. How about starting there and slurring all without a break, matching every tone and dynamic in *pp*? Then, again begin transposing up a half step, each one becoming more challenging until you reach E Major? As you go, jot down all of these into your staff paper booklet, as you'll want to refer to it again and again. This is what I mean by taking each excerpt and developing your own personalized warm up, based on the challenges you face most given the required excerpts for a particular audition.

By the time you reach practice time for the actual excerpt, you'll be amazed at how much better you sound, and how much more control you'll have almost immediately! As you're developing this, also begin each day this week with your "useful warm-up."

THE "NAUGHTY LIST"

Open up your audition booklet, with blank staff paper nearby, plus something to take a few notes on. Begin by playing through the entire list. You're not trying for perfection at this point, you're just reading through the entire list to get a feel for all of the excerpts. Some of them will come to you quite easily, having prepared them at some point in your recent past, and some will be quite difficult, needing much attention. Those needing much attention, that are quite far out of your grasp at this first reading, must be written down on a separate list. I call this the "naughty list." Hopefully this list will not be too overwhelming for the first reading, and it need not include entire excerpts, only specific measures where trouble lurks. I'm not talking about excerpts that you don't play perfectly at this point, I'm talking about the ones that you stumble heartily through, can't even play close to the advised tempo, or where you can't control the sound quality or dynamic at all. Don't worry if this list tends to be a bit lengthy at first, as it will get shorter almost immediately, and there is such a sense of triumph when an excerpt finally gets wiped from the "naughty list"! Following this "useful warm-up" that takes place first every day this week, then insert diligent and focused practice time on this naughty list!

INDEX CARDS

Grab your deck of blank index cards and a pen. On each card, you'll write one excerpt only. In the case of *Leonore No. 3*, for example, use one index card to write **LEONORE OPENING**, and another card to write **LEONORE SOLO**. I do the same for *Daphnis and Chloe* for each section that will be required. In the case of an entire symphony, or a symphony with several movements listed, use one card for each movement. I also use an index card for the required concerto on the list. If there is more than one movement listed, use one card per movement. Now count the number of cards in your deck, and divide that number by 6. This matches the number of days in a week, minus 1 (to be explained later). A typical audition can have an estimate of anywhere from 18-40 cards in the deck.

THE CHOICE

Remember, you have *chosen* to take this audition. From this moment on, it is imperative to keep all the voices in your head in check by filling yourself with all positive talk and messages:

> "I love this list!"
>
> "I'm excited to begin preparing all of this music!"
>
> "This is a great opportunity for me to improve, and I'm up to the task!"

Be aware of *any* negativity that may creep into your thoughts and out of your mouth, and take the opportunity to immediately change it into something positive. Apply this positivity to all texts, Facebook posts, tweets, etc. that you write in the next 6 weeks as well. Keep everything positive! *This will help you reach the finals more than you may ever know or believe in at this moment!*

WEEK 6 SUMMARY

As Week 6 comes to a close you will have:
1) Assembled all of your equipment
2) Made 3 audition booklets
3) Made a listening list for your portable music player
4) Written all the excerpt names on individual index cards
5) Cleared your schedule to the best of your ability from now until audition day
6) Picked out and kept in your possession your "mental" training book(s), along with a journal to jot down notes as you read them
7) Developed your own "useful" warm up, focused on this particular audition's challenges, and have begun putting this into play each day
8) Played through the entire audition list
9) Identified your "naughty list" and begun working diligently to familiarize yourself with the music on that list
10) Become aware of your thoughts and inner voices, so you stay positive about all areas around this audition

WEEK 5

During Week 5 you will continue beginning every day with your useful warm-up, followed by your naughty list. It's hard to determine how long these two daily tasks will take, as it depends completely on the level at which you began. The new auditioner will have a lengthy naughty list, and at first this can take several hours of practice all on its own. Even seasoned auditioners may find that their naughty list can take anywhere from a half hour to two hours in these beginning weeks. Don't be discouraged. This is why you have "respectfully declined" other tasks, as these first few weeks require quite a bit of your time. After completing these two tasks each day, it's time to put your index cards into play.

SHUFFLE, DRAW, AND PRACTICE!

Now that you've assembled your index cards, counted, and divided by 6, it's time to shuffle the cards Vegas style, and randomly draw the number of cards you came up with. Let's assume you began with a total of 30 excerpt cards, so you've now randomly drawn 5 from the deck.

The 5 you have drawn are your "task for the day" for each day in Week 5. These are the only excerpts you'll practice in that day, and the next day you will draw five more, and so on, through the 6th day when you finish up the deck. You are *not* allowed to put any cards back into the deck once you've drawn it, and you must finish your practice on that card (and all cards drawn) the day you draw it!

Since you won't return to any given excerpt for at least 6 more days, you must do what I call "nitty gritty" practicing on each one. This is the task that is so tempting to cheat on! I've drawn many a card I just *don't* feel like dealing with that day, but having the discipline to practice any card drawn, no matter what, will really benefit you in this program and in the end.

THE "NITTY GRITTY" PRACTICE METHOD

Once you've drawn your cards for the day, it's time to strip down those excerpts in a way that you'll attack the three most important elements required to reach the Finals in an audition. Ask any musician on a committee to come up with what they look for in preliminary rounds, and you'll hear these 6 words over and over again: "Play in Time, Play in Tune!" It sounds basic, but I guarantee the majority of candidates out there do NOT execute these two elements in the audition. Add in a third element of musical expression, and you've got it made!

Musical expression is a very broad term, so I'd like to clarify what it means in terms of "nitty gritty" work. You must play musically at an audition, which means every phrase must have meaning and intent. Each person's intent may vary, but it must be there. Study the composer and the style to find your intent, then be sure this is conveyed convincingly as you record and listen to playback. There are often many musical expression marks already printed in the music. As you prepare, be sure all of these markings, from dynamics to shadings are also all conveyed convincingly.

That is where the "nitty gritty" practice method comes to your aid. What I consider the "nitty gritty" involves isolating and practicing rhythm, intonation, and musical expression, your three most important elements, separately.

Now, set up your recording device and begin the first "mock" audition. Set up your excerpts in the order of cards drawn. Play through each excerpt in order, while recording just as you'd play them in the audition. This means no stopping and no distractions. Do not expect perfection in your mock at this stage! Remember this is merely a training exercise, and be as positive and accepting of your mock performance as you can possibly be. The excerpts on your naughty list will also come into play, as your index card pile contains *all* the excerpts on this list. If an excerpt is particularly naughty (this is where I heartily cough up the words *Classical Symphony* or *Peter*) it may not be in your best interest to mock these up to tempo in these early weeks. I highly suggest mocking them as perfectly as possible at a slower tempo. How much slower depends on your individual level, but one thing I can tell you for sure is that you're not doing yourself any favors by practicing in mistakes by going too fast at *any* point of your preparation. You'll still have the ability to check rhythm relationships and pitch in playback at the tempo that is right for you during this week.

You will now use this mock recording for the ensuing study and "nitty gritty" practice session. This one mock audition recording will now serve as the basis for your practice on this day, and you will use the same recording as you review each of the 3 stages of "nitty gritty," one at a time.

LET'S BEGIN WITH RHYTHM

For example, let's assume your first drawn and recorded excerpt was **LEONORE SOLO**. Grab your music, a pencil, and your metronome. Since you can pretty much guess your desired tempo, (for this excerpt I use ♩ =126-132), begin by turning the metronome click on at that tempo, then set your recording device to begin playback. The tricky part lies in lining up the metronome click that has been established with the already recorded track right at the start, or a few clicks into the excerpt. For this, I turn the metronome dial quickly to match the given beat, then immediately back to my tempo so that they begin to line up. This takes a bit of practice, but trust me, you will soon become an expert at this!

Once the click lines up, it's imperative that you trust the click to hear if what you recorded stays as steady as the true metronome click. A variance of one click up or down from your original tempo is fine and even expected, but if you're adjusting at 2 clicks above or below to stay together with your recorded track, then you are *not* playing rhythmically enough! ("Play in Time!")

At first listen, I always enjoy watching the look of pure horror flash across a student's face when they hear how far off their actual rhythm is when they thought they were actually playing perfectly in time! I only say this because I clearly remember the first few times I used this method myself, and my own look of pure horror and disbelief! Take note of where the biggest (to even the smallest) variances occur, and mark your part if you feel it's necessary; then practice with the metronome on, being aware of where your discrepancies on your recording occurred. Now turn the metronome off and practice again. Then practice again using only the light, not the click from the metronome. Another useful tool is the phone app called "Metronome" which looks like the old-style triangular box, with a pendulum that swings back and forth to a desired tempo. It is extremely good training to play the excerpts while watching the pendulum, but with the sound turned off. It acts almost like a conductor, and I believe this helps you internalize good rhythm. Repeat this process on the same excerpt over and over until you're coming *much* closer to playing perfectly in rhythm — *it really works!* This also works particularly well for any excerpt requiring a quick breath in tempo. We often think we haven't lost any time on the breath, but the only way to be absolutely sure is if your recorded track lines up with the metronome on playback, hence the breath taking place in time. *I cannot stress how important this is in an audition!*

NEXT IS INTONATION

Using the same recording of the excerpts you've already made to check your rhythm, now evaluate your intonation. Make sure your playback device has some sort of speaker and is close to your tuner, so the tuner can accurately pick up the pitch from your recording. Use your pencil to mark any notes that were out of tune in this excerpt. This works especially well for the slower excerpts. On fast excerpts, it's often difficult to evaluate every note, but it's easy to see if the high and loud passages all register sharp, or soft passages register as flat. For example, if *Peter and the Wolf* is all registering sharp, you'll need to adjust! If ends of notes and phrases appear flat or sharp on the tuner, you'll also need to adjust. These can be quite important, as they resonate in a hall after you have left the note, and you want to be sure they resonate in tune!

Make a mental note and mark your part if necessary, then practice over and over with careful attention to the particular places your playback was not in tune, using your tuner. Tuners do not lie! They are painfully accurate, and every effort must be made to have as perfect intonation as possible on each excerpt on your list. Use your ears as well, as in playback you'll hear your intonation much more clearly then when you are actually playing.

At a flute audition I sat on the committee for, we had heard about 65 candidates and passed very few, mostly due to poor rhythm or intonation. After the last candidate had left the stage and was well out of earshot, one of our committee members yelled out in a disgruntled and frustrated voice, "Playing in tune is NOT optional!" He voiced the frustration all of us on the committee shared at that moment, and we all had to giggle just a little. However, keep that disgruntled voice in your head as you prepare… "Playing in tune is NOT optional!"

At this point, you're still working on the first excerpt you've drawn from your deck. You are beginning to realize why the "I respectfully decline" comes in very handy!

EXPRESSION

Look closely at every marking on the page in the excerpt you just played. Treat it like the old game of "I spy"! "I spy a diminuendo" – did you *hear* a diminuendo on your recording? "I spy a *ff*" – did you *hear ff*, or just *f*? And one of my favorites, "I spy an accent" – did you actually *hear* an accent?

Being able to accurately and convincingly demonstrate to a committee the actual markings the composer put into the music is a skill that gets noticed and applauded by any committee, because it is so rarely achieved. Closely and realistically evaluate your ability to do this as you listen to this third pass on your playback.

The second part of this evaluation has to do with phrasing. You must first ask yourself what you intend with each musical phrase. Where does the phrase go to? Where are the appoggiaturas? What musical intention do you have for each phrase? Then, as you listen to your playback, evaluate if you once again actually *hear* the phrase the way you intended it. This can be extremely surprising. I always have a definite phrasing and musical intention in mind, believing strongly in it, and in my ability to be convincing with it. However at times on playback, I can't hear these intentions *at all!* I'm often shocked at the blandness of the phrase I thought I'd convincingly just played. You know what to do – rethink, practice again, re-evaluate, until what you intend matches what you actually *hear*, but more importantly, what a committee sitting in the hall will hear.

When you've finished these 3 tasks with the first excerpt, begin playback of the second excerpt from your "mock" audition, the second card in your divided up stack of excerpts for the day. Repeat and follow the steps above for each excerpt that you're responsible for that day (the number will vary because of the total number of excerpts on the list divided by 6).

You can switch the order of the three evaluations (rhythm, intonation, musical expression) if you need some variety. What you absolutely *cannot* do is switch out a drawn card for another if you do not like the excerpt you have drawn! *A card drawn is a card practiced!! No cheating!* This card system keeps you honest and accountable, so by audition day every single excerpt on your list is equally at the highest level possible.

This takes time, especially for longer audition lists. Week 5 will be intense and extremely time consuming, but very rewarding. You have to trust the system, as once you've recorded your one "mock" runthrough and really worked on the card drawn, it will not appear again in the rotation until Week 4. But you'll absolutely retain the work and progress made on every single excerpt this week. This is a valuable tool, as it gives you permission to really tackle the list in an organized and efficient way, rather than being overwhelmed by the immense amount of work that randomly tackling the list would entail.

Following is how I might mark up the Leonore solo in the 3 "nitty gritty" playbacks.

1. Rhythm
2. Intonation
3. Musical Expression

With DSO colleagues Donald Baker oboe, Jennifer Volk guest flutist, and Jeffery Zook piccolo
photo credit: Victor Mangona

YOUR MENTAL GAME

> "No matter how we approach life, completely committing ourselves to whatever we do is essential. If you have committed yourself, and you have given it your best shot, then that's all you can do." — Billie Jean King

> "Set your compass in a chosen direction, and then focus your attention and efforts completely on the journey of preparation. A successful journey becomes your destination and is where your real accomplishment lies." — Coach John Wooden

(Footnotes 2 & 3)

I've kept a journal of meaningful quotes for as long as I can remember. When I read or study one of the mental toughness training books, I keep my journal close by. Some books have so many quotes that speak to me, I find myself stopping to write incessantly! Looking back at this point over a 25-year career, I'm truly glad I've done this, as I have an easy reference to return to over and over as I practice, prepare, and inspire myself for the next event. By now you will have chosen the book(s) you will be reading over the next 5 weeks. Be sure you've set aside time to read every day, taking notes as you go along. Keep in mind, this event you're preparing for is a *triathlon*, and it's equally important for you to be equally trained in three areas, not just one, to be successful! I'm so often asked by musicians training for auditions, "How do I even begin to prepare mentally?" Begin with your quote journal!

DAY 7, THE EXTRA DAY

You may have wondered why, after shuffling all the excerpt cards, I asked you to divide by 6 instead of 7. The work required on each of these 6 days is intense and extremely time consuming if you stay true to actual "nitty gritty" practice. Many times it has gotten to be 1 or 2am, and I still have 1 or 2 cards left on the table that day to stay on track. Knowing there's an extra day built into the schedule each week is very helpful!

In a perfect world, you can get through the actual number of cards drawn in all 6 days, but in our busy and demanding lives, this is not always the case. However, you also cannot abuse the system, by shifting too many excerpts to day 7! Realistically, 5 or 6 excerpts per day is probably the most one can do "nitty gritty" work on, so please don't leave more than that left over if you can possibly help yourself.

Day 7 can also be very helpful for audition lists with many complete parts on them. For example, many flute lists contain complete *Suite No. 2 from Daphnis*, complete *Peter and the Wolf*, complete Brahms *Symphony No. 2*, complete Prokofiev *Classical Symphony*, and so on. It's impossible to put all those tutti sections onto individual index cards, yet you still must be totally prepared for every note on the list. For this kind of audition list, I try to diligently stick to the plan to finish the nitty gritty work over 6 days, then reserve Day 7 for the complete parts. I look through and practice all the tutti passages I haven't included on index cards, or divide them in half, knowing that on the following Day 7 I'll practice the other half. As I do this, I make a note as to what I can't play well yet, and will possibly add just that small section to an index card and shuffle it into the mix over the next two weeks. This way you won't feel overwhelmed and will also be completely prepared come audition day!

WEEK 5 SUMMARY

As Week 5 comes to a close you will have:

1) Solidified your "useful" warm up, used it every day, and gained much more strength and control in your playing even before touching the excerpts
2) Tackled your "naughty list" daily, possibly even being able to take one of them off that list as they become familiar and tamed
3) Recorded and practiced every single excerpt on the audition list with superb attention to detail in the 3 most important areas, rhythm, intonation and musical expression
4) Spent some time playing through and analyzing all of the tutti sections required for this audition
5) Begun your "quote journal," having picked out and begun studying your mental preparation book(s)
6) Kept your inner voices in check, with all your positive talk and thoughts replacing any negativity with something positive

WEEK 4

You are well on your way and still have one whole month until audition day!

Once again, begin each practice day with your useful warm-up and naughty list. I have a feeling some of the excerpts on your naughty list will get the boot this week! But don't be surprised or discouraged if this start to your day is still taking quite a bit of time.

Shuffle your entire deck of audition cards, and once again divide by 6 and draw. You'll proceed in exactly the same way as in Week 5, beginning each day by recording a "mock" play-through of all of the excerpts drawn, in the order you drew them. However, you'll find that this week you're already beginning with much better discipline in the areas of intonation, rhythm, and musical expression, and closer to where you want to end up by audition time. It will take a little less time to carefully prepare each excerpt than in Week 5. No matter how tempting it may be, do *not* cheat and substitute excerpts drawn for other excerpts you'd rather play or practice. I only stress this because I know first-hand how extremely tempting this can be!

Those of you who have seen the movie "Toy Story" will appreciate this analogy: I feel like the index cards are the little green aliens in Pizza Planet, who randomly get chosen by "The Claw"! The Claw rules and when chosen, you must go! I'll never forget one time when I was having my young son choose cards for me (we did this often!); that particular day, I just did NOT feel like tackling one of the cards he had drawn. I looked at the card, looked at him, passed it back and said, "Oh, please just pull another one." He immediately barked at me, "That's NOT how it works, Mom!" This really made me smile, and I knew that my task had been already chosen!

By the end of this week, you will once again have carefully and meticulously practiced every single excerpt on your audition list.

CHECK YOUR COURSE

It is now time to "check your course." Any great race car driver, cyclist, and even pro golfer knows better than to step into competition day without ever checking out the route or course they'll compete on. We, as musicians, must do the same. Our "course" involves the hall we'll audition in, the players who'll most likely be on our Audition Committee, and the Music Director of the orchestra we're auditioning for. The internet is an amazing resource for all these things. Don't be afraid to take some initiative in seeking out valuable information! I personally would never be taken aback if I received an email that read something like this:

SUBJECT: Audition Inquiry

Hello Ms. Sparrow,

I will soon be taking the audition for (any position) in the Detroit Symphony. As part of my preparation, I hope you would not mind answering a couple of questions. Since I am unfamiliar with Orchestra Hall and would like to do my best at the audition, could you please tell me your opinion on the acoustics while playing from the stage there? For screened rounds, do you place your screen on the stage in front of the candidates or in the hall in front of the committee? Do we receive a private warm up room before our number is called? I appreciate your time and thank you in advance for this helpful information.

Respectfully,
Iam the Mostprepared

I would respond in the following way:

re: Audition Inquiry

Dear Iam the,

I would be happy to answer your questions. Orchestra Hall has wonderful acoustics! However, I've found that in flute auditions, what is played onstage becomes quite blurred in the Hall where our committee sits. Therefore, the candidate needs to play extremely articulately on stage. For instance, Mendelssohn's *Scherzo* played quite normally can sound almost slurred in our hall, therefore it's best to exaggerate short articulation in Orchestra Hall. Dynamics are tricky as well, as the hall graciously picks up even the softest of sounds and enhances it to sound quite a bit louder than you'd imagine. A true *pp* on the page will need to be expertly and very softly executed on the stage to sound as a true *pp* in our Hall. Our screen extends the full width of the stage and is placed at the front of the stage. The candidate plays from the center of the stage toward the front, a few feet behind the screen. You'll receive your own private warm up room when "on deck" to take the stage. Best of luck in the upcoming audition!

Sharon Sparrow
Detroit Symphony, Assistant Principal Flute

Check the orchestra's website. They may do live webcasts, as we do in the DSO, which are very valuable in gaining many insights for the audition. Research the players in the section you're auditioning for. Where did they study? Are there any clues that may help in your preparation? What's coming up in their season? What have they just finished playing? This may give you a slight clue if sightreading is indicated on your audition list.

Who is the Music Director? Are there any webcasts available with that conductor that you can watch? Recordings they've made that you could listen to? Are there other orchestras this Director may have guest conducted that you know players in, to get some information? For instance, you may be auditioning for the Seattle Symphony, where you do not know any of the musicians. But through research, you learn that Seattle's Music Director often conducts the Pittsburgh Symphony where you may have a good friend in the flute section. Bend that friend's ear to learn what characteristics this music director favors. You're just gathering as much information as possible, and you'll use this collection of small details to create the big picture for your mock training and ultimately your live audition.

A very important part of your preparation should include Visualization exercises. If you have a mental image of the hall, and even of the Committee, you'll be even more able to create the most realistic picture in your head when you visualize the audition experience. I personally know an audition candidate who went as far as searching the internet for pictures of all the key players he thought would be on his audition committee. He then copied and enlarged their pictures, printed them out, and cut each head shot out. He then set them up behind a screen and also without a screen to practice many mock auditions. This is certainly creative yet extreme, but guess what – this candidate won a Principal wind position in a major orchestra! Keep in mind, preliminary rounds in auditions rarely last more than 5 or 6 minutes. The more times you accurately visualize this experience, you will increase your odds exponentially for an extremely successful experience for those brief and very real moments on the stage.

MOCK AUDITIONS, FORMAL AND INFORMAL

When I was in high school I had the opportunity to pick an elective in my senior year. Since I was totally consumed in music classes, I decided to try something completely new, Aviation! For 16 weeks, we studied every tiny aspect of aviation from a 600-page resource book that I found both daunting and fascinating. Our teacher was a pilot, and he was so knowledgeable and passionate about flying planes. A huge part of this class was "simulator training." In our classroom there was an airplane simulator with all of the knobs, throttles, buttons, switches, etc., placed exactly as they would be on a private plane. Each student spent countless hours in this simulator, repeatedly drilling takeoff and landing, the two most important parts of any flight.

The "final" for this class was the reason I signed up – we were taken to the nearby airport, and each of us took a turn piloting a small private plane! (with the instructor and other licensed pilot in the cockpit as well). Although our turn lasted only about 10 minutes (about the same amount of time as an audition round), those 10 minutes were so thrilling and unforgettable! They could also have been terrifying and demoralizing. However, by the time we were in the actual plane, we had trained in our simulator SO many times, it didn't feel much different at all. I felt I already knew exactly what to do, how to react, and therefore had the freedom to just *enjoy the experience as it was taking place.*

I totally can equate this to the "mock audition" part of training for an audition. It's simulator training, so try to make it as real as possible. After all, your goal for the actual audition is to be at a point where you can just enjoy the experience as it is taking place!

Remember, this is a triathlon you're preparing for. Mock auditions require as much of your attention as practicing your excerpts and your mental training! You've already begun *informal* mock auditions in Week 5, and this will continue in the ensuing weeks. Each day that you drew excerpts, it was your task to begin by recording those excerpts before beginning nitty gritty practice. The more seriously you take these informal mocks every day, the better you will perform on audition day. Stay honest and focused for this each day, beginning to find a rhythm and routine to this important element of preparation.

In this Week 4, however, you must set up 3 *formal* mock auditions to take place in the coming weeks. I've found it is best to space these out by having one each in weeks 3, 2, and 1. These formal mock auditions involve a committee that you've assembled, coerced, sought out, bribed, etc. It's very important to set these up in 3 contrasting locations, at least one being in as similar a place as your upcoming audition and with 3 different sets of listeners. Include at least one player from each different section of the orchestra (but NOT a flutist!). Flutists are all trained to listen to excerpts in a particular way similar to your own listening. Other instrumentalists will hear many things that are not noticed by listening flutists. And honestly, your audition committee will be made up of a majority of non-flutists!

It is very valuable to set up one of your formal mock auditions away from your area if possible. Maybe there's a flutist in a nearby or easily accessible city that you can set up a mock audition with. This is so valuable because you'll mimic the experience of adding travel to just playing the excerpts, which is likely what you'll do for the real audition. See what it's like to travel, stay somewhere unfamiliar, play for someone you do not know but really respect or even better, are intimidated by. Discover what is both unsettling and inspiring about this experience and put it in your bank to use at the real audition.

I clearly remember fearfully contacting by email a very famous flutist whom I had never met but was totally inspired by for many years to prepare for an upcoming audition. To my surprise and delight, he graciously responded and reserved a date in his busy schedule to hear my excerpts. I traveled out of town, reserved a hotel the night before, and went to play for him the next morning. His comments were invaluable as was the whole experience! I was more nervous playing for him than I would have been for any Committee of any audition. I learned a great deal from that experience alone, and strongly encourage you to do the same!

Again, the internet is very resourceful in helping you find and contact someone you'd like to play for. A well-written and respectful email will almost always generate a gracious response from anyone in our field. Be prepared, though, to pay the fee this person charges for a coaching, and make clear in your email that you are offering to pay for their time and not asking them to hear you for free.

After each of these formal mocks, take a few minutes to write in your journal as many details as you can remember of the experience. As you accumulate data, you will refer back to this time and time again to help you produce the best results.

You will want to begin thinking about travel arrangements at the beginning of Week 4. Many airlines offer a discounted fare if booked 30 days in advance. Personally I use websites that compare fees, and I have enjoyed the benefits of alternative bed & breakfast lodging as well as hotels. By taking advantage of the many great alternative deals available, the chances of hearing many flutists playing the same excerpts as you in the hotels suggested by the auditioning orchestra are slim to none! Be sure you confirm that you will be allowed to practice in the space you have rented, and also read reviews! If you go the hotel route, many hotels have no problem with you using an unoccupied conference room for practicing. It's amazing what you can achieve if you *just ask*!

KNOW AND LOVE

Since by this point your naughty list should be getting shorter, and it will take less time to nitty gritty practice each excerpt, you'll have time to begin another important aspect of your preparation during this week.

It is now time to research half of the excerpts on the list and play through each of them with a recording. Since your playlist is already in place (see Week 6), you are ready to go! Depending on the list, you may prefer to divide it into thirds instead of half. There will be time over three weeks to accomplish this task, though I usually prefer to just do it in two.

By research, I mean know something about the excerpts, the composers, the time period, and the style. What is the meaning behind the beautiful and passionate solo in Brahms' *Symphony No. 4*? What do you know about Beethoven when he was composing *Leonore Overture No. 3*? What was the opera about? What was the style of playing intended in Bach's *St. Matthew Passion*? Translate and memorize the text in the "Aus Liebe" movement.

Learn to really *understand* first, and then *love* what you are playing. With understanding comes a deeper meaning, and this always translates itself into your playing.

I recently had the extreme pleasure of playing the entire concert version of Strauss's opera *Salome* with the DSO. Before rehearsals began, I studied the entire score with a recording, and also read a translation of the complete libretto. By the point in the opera that the "Dance of the Seven Veils" appears, I was literally immersed in the scene and the drama. My heart was filled and racing with emotion. Although for this performance I was covering the 3rd Flute part, I wanted to practice playing the famous flute solo at home. I was shocked, amazed, and delighted that by following every measure, phrase, and word of the opera up to the point of this solo entrance, I played the solo entirely differently than I ever had before! There was new-found understanding and emotion behind every note I played! And then I pretty much kicked myself for never taking the time to do this before all of my past auditions!

At a recent audition where I was on the committee, one candidate really stood out from the others in the Brahms 4 flute solo. I later found out this candidate had thoroughly done her research on the whole symphony, the composer, and that particular solo. It made a phenomenal difference in a solo that a committee hears almost 100 times in an audition! Know how each excerpt fits into the piece as a whole. These excerpts are all really so much more than just small snippets of notes! I've sat on many audition committees, and the players who really know and understand the meaning behind the excerpts, the style, and the composers, always stand out from the pack. The time you spend on this exercise may be the small difference that pushes you out of the semis and into the finals!

"The aim of art is not to represent the outward appearance of things but their inward significance."

— Aristotle

TRUST THE SYSTEM

By the time you reach this point, three full weeks of your training are complete and you're getting ready for a formal mock to take place next week already. You may be thinking that by doing the nitty gritty practicing and drawing of cards, that you only hit each excerpt once a week and begin to panic that that is simply not enough. I ask that you trust the system at this point!

Over the next three weeks you will be rotating each excerpt into the mix many more times, and the value you've gained from this way of practicing to this point will not fail you! Your first mock may not be perfect, but that is not the point just yet. I've also carefully crafted out the weeks so you won't be bored or tired of any of the excerpts on audition day, but rather prepared and excited. If you're staying true to tackling your naughty list first, and then your nitty gritty, I can guarantee you'll achieve the results you're hoping for.

WEEK 4 SUMMARY

As Week 4 comes to a close you will have:

1) Continued with your "useful" warm up followed by attack of the "naughty list" to begin each day
2) Joyously booted some excerpts OFF your "naughty list" while continuing to practice those other "naughty" ones still on it
3) Used your "nitty gritty" practice method on all the excerpts on the list, always beginning with a "home mock" audition of the excerpts you've drawn. At this point, your best friends remain your recording device, tuner, and metronome!
4) Done your homework by researching the hall you are playing in, the possible committee that will be listening to you, and the current Music Director
5) Set up your 3 formal mock auditions
6) Looked into travel arrangements for the audition, including a place to stay that allows you to practice
7) Played through half of your audition list with a recording, going beyond just the excerpt and including either the whole movement or the whole piece
8) Researched half of the excerpts to have a better understanding of what you're playing and to gain more respect and love for each excerpt
9) Continued reading and studying your mental training book(s) while keeping notes in your journal
10) Kept all of your thoughts and self-talk in check to remain ONLY positive!
    - I am becoming very excited about this audition day
    - I am feeling better prepared than ever before
    - I feel connected to the excerpts and the meaning behind each one in a new and exciting way

WEEK 3

> "The heights by great men reached and kept, were not attained by sudden flight. But they, while their companions slept, were tolling upward in the night."
>
> — Henry Wadsworth Longfellow

Congratulations! While others have been sleeping, you have been tolling upwards, tackling your naughty list and diligently doing your nitty gritty work. You have worked extremely hard, and I am quite sure by this point you're beginning to feel a sense of accomplishment as well as new strength that comes from the inside out, from the work you have completed. There is no other way to have this feeling of inner strength than having done the work.

Therefore, in Week 3, set up a small reward for yourself. Do something that makes you happy, with or without your flute! When my son was little, he was obsessed with Winnie the Pooh. I loved reading those books to him and loved how Christopher Robin would spontaneously set up a "hero party." We began to spontaneously do the same in our house, to much delight! If you've prepared well these last 3 weeks and really have stuck to the program, then you deserve a "hero party" some time in this week! You will have time because by this point, I guarantee your naughty list will be shorter, and your nitty gritty work on every excerpt will take much less time. You'll be able to draw and successfully complete anywhere from 2 to 4 more index cards in a day, therefore leaving a little extra time for other things.

Still begin each practice day with your useful warm-up. Have you added to it since the first week? Have you thought about tweaking it to address specific challenging issues that have come up while practicing the excerpts in the past three weeks? Keep your staff paper handy, and be sure to always intelligently be adding or subtracting things that will be useful to YOU, personally. Follow your warm up once again with your naughty list. I am quite sure these are all progressing nicely and becoming much more familiar to you.

It is still important to continue your nitty gritty practicing, but since you've become much better at this, increase the number of cards you draw each day. If you were previously drawing say 4 cards, try 6 or 7. This is a rewarding feeling! It will also make your "daily home mock" a little closer to what the actual round will be like. It's amazing to me that no matter which 6 or 7 excerpt cards are randomly drawn, it always seems like it could be a likely round at the audition!

You will continue the "know and love" that began in Week 4. Play through the other half (or third, depending on list size) of your excerpts with a recording, and do your research! I always find I play the excerpts just a little bit differently after playing them through with a recording. Auditioning is a lonely endeavor, and probably the only time you'll be standing on that stage all by yourself. This task enables me to feel like rather than being on stage alone, I have the entire "virtual orchestra" playing with me in my head. Not only is it a very nice feeling, but it is always very apparent to your committee!

FRIEND CHECK

You've been working very hard on your own up to this point and are becoming extremely prepared with your excerpts. It's time to enlist some help or some company for a portion of your practice time if possible. Grab a friend, colleague, or I have even used my children for this in the past. Their job is to check your pitch and rhythm *while* you play the excerpts using those most familiar tools, your tuner and metronome.

For example, play the opening of *Leonore* and have them watch the needle on the tuner. Have them call you out when you stray out of the perfect or near-perfect zone. Play again. Did they call you out again? Try to do this until they give you the ok that you have played *in tune*. Your actual audition committee members more than likely will be doing this exact thing from the other side of the screen, but instead of calling you out, they will rule you out!

You can do the same exercise with rhythm using the metronome. Play the Mendelssohn *Scherzo* for example, having them holding the metronome with the click on. After you start playing and a few clicks go by, have them switch to the light only, eliminating the click. Again, be sure they're willing to call you out if you don't remain *in tempo* with the metronome light. This way, you'll also know exactly where in the excerpt you begin to fall off the rhythm track. Somehow, my children took great delight in these tasks and actually looked forward to the practice sessions when I would enlist their help! They also loved being the ones able to "draw the cards" from the deck for a practice session. Remember, *pitch* and *rhythm* must be nearly perfect to advance out of the Preliminary round, so your attention to these two elements are always of the utmost importance while preparing.

A LITTLE MORE DIFFICULT, PLEASE

You know most of the excerpts quite well by now. So, I urge you to take the excerpts that challenge you and make them even more difficult! For instance, are you having trouble with the breathing in Debussy's *Faune*? Take it even slower! Play the whole phrase in only one breath. Do the same with *Scherzo* by eliminating one of the two obvious breaths. Push yourself to only take ONE breath instead of two! Use transposition. Take the opening scale of the *Daphnis* solo and keep transposing it up one half step at a time.

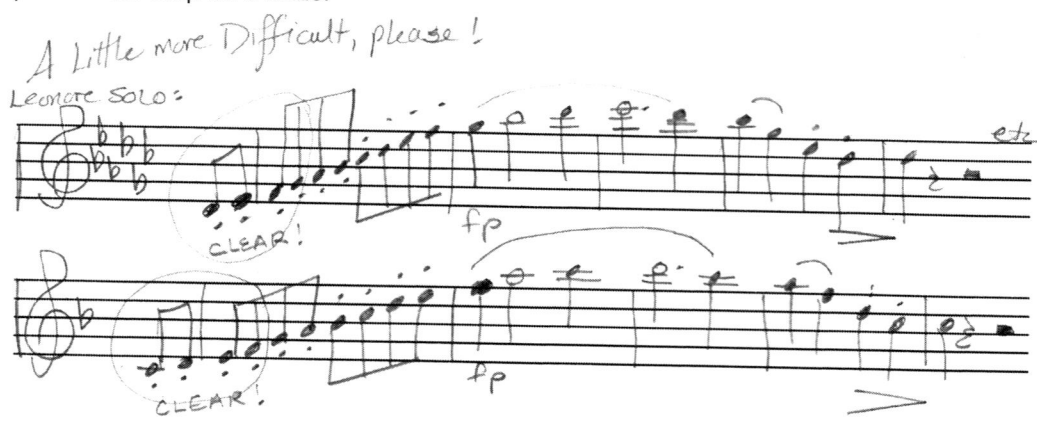

Start at ♪ = 116 and gradually progress to ♪ = 88.

I recently saw a post on someone's Facebook page who had just won an audition. In a practice session, they recorded the opening solo of *Faune*, playing not once through in one breath, but three times in succession in only one breath! Although not the most musical example I've heard, it was impressive and inspiring. I don't think that candidate had to ever give a second thought to running out of air in that excerpt and could concentrate in the audition on playing beautiful music instead. Try this on a couple of excerpts per day for a few minutes. You'll be amazed that when you return to the original, it will seem so much easier and even effortless! This always works.

YOUR FORMAL MOCK AUDITION

It is imperative that you perform one of your formal mocks during this week. Try to create a scenario as close as possible to the real audition. Note the surroundings, time of day, what you have eaten, what your pre-audition ritual is, what you are wearing, what is your self-talk before, during and after. Take a moment and jot these down in your audition journal. What you learn from this experience is extremely useful. The more experience and knowledge you have, the quicker you'll be able to get into a relaxed and focused state for the event itself. Don't be focused on being perfect at this mock. This is part of the learning process and a chance to test out not only your skills to this point, but also your mental game as well. It is so important that you bring *intensity* into the equation for this mock, and all mock auditions (and even many practice sessions) going forward. Get psyched up for this! Do not be complacent.

THE "VIRTUAL MOCK"

I only recently discovered how useful the addition of this technique to my preparation could be. Based on sports training books, I decided to add in a "virtual mock." This is how it works: once again draw 6 (or so) random cards from the deck. But instead of playing them this time, find a quiet place to sit. Begin by taking ten long, slow breaths with your eyes closed. As you breathe and relax, start to visualize yourself just offstage, about to walk onstage for your audition. Keep taking slow breaths and visualize yourself being calm, relaxed, yet excited to walk onto that stage. Feel your flute in your hands and how connected you are to it. See yourself almost grinning with excitement. Now visualize the walk onto the stage, turning toward the screen or committee, and raising your flute to your lips feeling completely calm and confident. Now picture yourself playing each of the excerpts you have drawn, one by one, hearing it come out effortlessly, flawlessly, musically! All the while, your eyes remain closed and your breaths are steady. See yourself enjoying the experience, being connected and focused with each new excerpt, hearing the beautiful sounds you are creating. After you have completed the last excerpt, hear the committee saying "thank you," and imagine the smiles on their faces. Take one last slow breath and see yourself walking confidently off of the stage. When you have reached backstage, open your eyes! This takes literally 6 to 9 minutes tops, and what you will gain from those few minutes will honestly surpass several hours of practicing! I understand that for many of us, this feels *extremely* unnatural, even silly, and it is easy to skip or avoid ever even trying this. I urge you to put your skepticism aside though, if only for 7 or 8 minutes per day. Stop what you are doing right now and go and try this!

SEEING IS BELIEVING

This old adage is always true! A large part of preparation is in setting a specific goal, (performing your absolute best at the audition) choosing a strategy to get there (following the 6-week plan), and then visualizing the outcome (walking off the stage feeling incredible; hearing the personnel manager call your number to advance; playing in the final round with complete ease, freedom, intensity and accuracy). *See* this in your mind so clearly that it is as if you are living it before it even happens! It's like watching a film that you wrote, starred in, produced and directed.

Every morning and night for more than 6 months leading up to the 1990 Wimbledon tournament, the legendary tennis player Martina Navratilova wrote out "I won Wimbledon in 1990" as if it had already happened, visualizing it over and over again. Was it any coincidence that she actually *won* Wimbledon that year?

Imagine yourself right at this spot, backstage at Orchestra Hall.
The screen in up, the carpet in place, the stage is set for your audition!

WEEK 3 SUMMARY

As Week 3 comes to a close you will have:

1) Treated yourself to a small reward for all of your hard work up to this point!
2) Continued with your "useful" warm up, reevaluating what is really most useful to YOU at this point in your preparation
3) Knocked a few more passages off of your "naughty list"
4) Done your "nitty gritty" practice for all of the excerpts, however, getting through many more in a day
5) Completed more research on the remaining excerpts from Week 4 and played them through with an orchestral recording
6) Performed one formal mock audition and jotted down helpful notes from the experience in your audition journal
7) Continued reading and studying your mental training book(s) while keeping notes in your journal, all the while keeping all of your thoughts and words positive
8) Enlisted a "friend check" for one or more practice sessions if possible
9) Found ways to make the challenging excerpts even more difficult for practice's sake
10) Tried a minimum of one "virtual mock" following all of the steps in this chapter

WEEK 2

By this point, you know the drill.

Begin with your "useful" warm up. It's been tweaked and revised, and the one you are using this week should be the one that you stick to right through Audition Day! There is value in having a ritual at this point for your audition day, and this will begin with your warm up.

Next, tackle those (hopefully) very few left on that naughty list. Don't worry if others have crept onto this list in the last two weeks, which can definitely happen. Stay focused and diligent and work those off of the list as well.

You can now draw quite a lot of cards, maybe even dividing your deck in two or three at this point for your recorded daily mock audition and "nitty gritty" practice. However, here's where we enhance the drill.

ACCESSING YOUR "FULL POTENTIAL SELF"

Your main focus up to this point has been on practicing, however, we must not forget that taking an audition is like a triathlon. You've been incorporating your swimming and biking training all along, but now it's time to get even more serious about them so these skills are equal to your practice preparation. This is often where most auditionees become stuck and confused, not knowing what or how to enhance the mental training skills needed. I was the first person to be skeptical of the methods I am about to share, being a very literal person, believing in much more tangible suggestions. However, I was extremely fortunate to have a very close and trusted friend who was once a professional flutist herself, having taken and been successful at many auditions, then giving up her career for one based in personal growth coaching for "full potential self" as well as energy coaching. She, herself uses the term "maybe a little too sci-fi" for some people, but together we've extracted some basics that have really changed the mental game for many of my students for auditions, recitals, presentations and life in general!

DRILL NO. 1

You've drawn your cards, and the next step is to record your home mock audition. STOP! Let's call this "getting grounded." Sit down and cross your left ankle over the right, and your right wrist over the left. Put the tip of your tongue on the roof of your mouth. Close your eyes. Now inhale for 4 counts through the nose, deep breaths. After the 4th breath, hold and count to 4. Next, exhale for 4 counts again through your nose. Stop after the exhale and count again to 4, repeating a brief word or phrase that is empowering to you, such as "limitless," or "purposeful." Make sure the tip of your tongue is still resting on the roof of your mouth. Repeat this pattern 3-6 times. After the last time, having ended with your empowering word, stand up slowly, approach your music stand, and begin your recorded mock. This exercise is known as a focus exercise. There is nothing more empowering than feeling focused and relaxed each and every time you play any mock audition for these next two weeks! The first few times you try this, it may seem very foreign and unnatural to you (I admit, it certainly did to me!), however after several times, you'll begin to realize that you actually ARE more focused and relaxed, reaping the benefits in your mock auditions from this exercise combined with your intense practice ritual to this point. On the other hand there is nothing more disappointing than to have put in hour upon hour of practice time, only to feel unfocused, distracted, negative or scattered for those all-important few minutes on the stage. Try it! You have virtually nothing to lose!!

DRILL NO. 2

Vitruvian Man stance. Vitruvian Man is a drawing by Leonardo da Vinci from the year 1490. The drawing depicts a man in two superimposed positions with his arms and legs apart and inscribed in a circle and square. Assume this same pose as Vitruvian Man, separating your legs and reaching your arms out to the side. (Left hand palm turned up, right hand palm turned down) While holding the pose, again put the tip of your tongue to the roof of your mouth. Breathe fully! Close your eyes and inhale slowly for 6 counts. Hold for 3. Exhale slowly for 6 counts. Repeat this cycle 3-6 times. As soon as you finish, pick up your flute. Now you are ready to play your mock. Note if you feel or play differently!

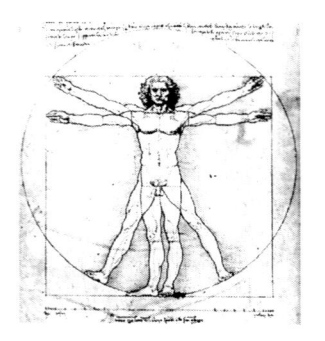

DRILL NO. 3

This is a focusing exercise, also used to energize you. Stand with your feet slightly apart. Bring your left hand across your body and grab your right earlobe, thumb on front of your earlobe. Cross your right hand always over the left and grab your left earlobe (thumb on front of earlobe). Put the tip of your tongue to the roof of your mouth. Close your eyes and breathe. Next inhale through your nose while bending your knees into a squat. Exhale through the nose while coming back up to standing. Repeat anywhere from 7 to 21 times. You are now both focused and energized! This is also a great little pick up anytime you're feeling sluggish, have long teaching days, etc!

To explore any of these ideas in Drills 1-3 further, I strongly encourage you to check out *www.sourcemovement.com/peakperformance* — I can promise you that this one click will give you a whole new edge for your next audition.

DRILL NO. 4

Power posing. I once watched an incredible TEDtalk with Social Psychologist Amy Cuddy. Her research and demonstrations on "power posing" were quite fascinating and useful. She incorporates ideas I've always believed in and used in teaching about how your posture, and how you stand, can actually have an effect on your performance, whether in speaking, interviewing, and more importantly, auditioning! Your posture can even change the levels of cortisone and testosterone levels in your brain. Amy Cuddy is easily found on the internet, and this can easily become your Drill No. 4! Honestly, what do you have to lose?

I'm certainly not suggesting that you try all four of these each time in succession. I only strongly encourage that you try each one, find one that possibly resonates with you, and stick to it until it becomes your familiar routine. Drills 1 and 4 can be easily incorporated *at* the audition without anyone noticing or even suspecting what you are doing. Drills 2 and 3 might be better incorporated in your warm-up room!

INTENSITY

If you look up the word "intensity" in the dictionary, you will find words such as strength, force, energy, and feeling. You've been practicing and mocking for weeks now. Audition day is closer and closer. It's time to make sure every mock audition has the all-important element of intensity! It's easy to fall into the trap of practicing and performing your mock auditions routinely, without bringing intensity to the task.

One of my favorite books is titled "Pressure Is A Privilege" by tennis champion Billie Jean King. In the book she states:

> "Preparation is the key to 'bringing' all of yourself. When match day arrives, it is always too late. If you do not practice with the same intensity that you plan to bring to the match, you will undermine your performance." [4]

Wow. After reading this statement, I realized I had certainly not been bringing all of myself *or* a high level of intensity to most of my mock auditions! With so much nitty gritty practice, you can lose your connection to the absolute intensity that must accompany your performance in mock and live auditions. Yes, trust your attention to detail, but play with passion and intent! Do NOT wait until audition day to begin knowing this feeling. Where is your extreme degree of strength, force, energy, or feeling? *Find* it and *use* it!

EXTREME MEASURES

As you may have already guessed, I am a huge sports fan. I tend to follow the careers of very successful athletes, watching them compete and reading their books. I feel music and sports are extremely connected. One of the many things I'm impressed by with top athletes is how they are never satisfied with doing only what is required. They train using extreme measures, always pushing the limits. They train tirelessly, both physically and mentally, trying to get a small edge over their competition. I feel musicians can learn a lot from competitive athletes.

One day, while reading about an athlete who had once again taken his training beyond the limits, it occurred to me that part of *my* training for audition day needed to include preparing for extremes. There's a lot that we *can* control about our audition, but also some things that we cannot. If we actually prepare for those things beyond our control, they are a lot less likely to frustrate, distract, and worst case, derail us in our all important few minutes onstage. Here are a few examples:

TEMPERATURE — I don't know about you, but it seems that almost every concert hall I've ever performed or auditioned in is either too cold or too hot. Some go as far as being absolutely freezing! If you always mock audition in a comfortable environment and you get onto a stage that's freezing for your audition, your instrument will react differently. Your keys will start spouting water at every turn! Your fingers will react differently. Things practiced with ease will suddenly seem awkward and difficult. If you've never practiced for this, your mind will most likely become distracted and unfocused.

However, if you've mocked in an extremely cold environment a few times, you'll learn how to negotiate your way through this. You'll take time to either swab out or use papers to collect excess water from your keys, knowing the feeling of doing this under pressure. You will *not* be distracted by this, because you'll absolutely know what to expect! The same applies for hot or humid halls. Take the time to mock in these extreme conditions so that you've practiced a successful plan of how to react and deal with this.

FOOD — In one early audition I had made it to the semi-finals... phew! It had been many hours since I'd eaten, and I was quite hungry. Not knowing how much time I'd have, I ventured out of the hall and grabbed the very first thing that sounded good, fast, and affordable. Frozen yogurt! Yum! I rushed back to the hall just in time to draw numbers for the next round. I drew #2. I was ushered to my warm up room, assembled my flute, only to find I could not achieve *any* sort of respectable sound! Try as I may, that frozen yogurt had pretty much frozen my lips and my throat, rendering my sound completely unacceptable. That was a very expensive mistake for me to make, as I couldn't execute well at all onstage and was not advanced past that round! Let my expensive lesson be your Lesson Learned.

Begin in this week finding foods that energize you, do not mess with your sound or embouchure, and can be readily available at an audition. Experiment with meals, learning how much and how far in advance eating works for you. Learn not only what to eat, but what *not* to eat! Experiment with mocks at different times of the day for the sole purpose of figuring this out. I find I play my best when I'm just a tiny bit hungry, and my worst when extremely full or on an empty stomach. Again, prepare and plan for these things to stay focused, not be distracted and to play your best!

ACOUSTICS — We are musicians. Sound is *very* important to us! Most of us practice mainly in the same location. We become very used to our sound in that location, whether it be a dry or live, dead or an enhancing acoustic. However, when we play our first notes on an unfamiliar stage, the sound we hear will most likely be new and very different from what we are used to. Learning to *not* react to what we hear is a very important skill to practice well before stepping onto that stage! Whether it's the best acoustic ever, or the most dead and unflattering sound we've ever heard coming back at us, we must *not* react emotionally.

One way to ensure this is to be sure to do your mocks in varying acoustical settings. Keeping your focus, especially in a very dead acoustic is a learned skill. Also, with some apps (such as Garage Band), you can actually change the acoustic on your playback to create extremes. Hearing your sound in these extremes will be helpful as you prepare for an unfamiliar stage or room.

I know from experience how different and distracting these acoustics can be. One important audition for me took place in a ballet studio with a strange floor and black curtains completely surrounding the room. The very first phrase of my Mozart concerto elicited my internal reaction, "What in the #U(!&@&?!" It was difficult to adjust and recover after that, which was a *Lesson Well Learned* for me.

On the complete other side of the spectrum, I remember an audition on a very live stage where I fell so in love with how I sounded on that stage I couldn't concentrate on anything else! Another *Lesson Learned!*

By *preparing* in your mock auditions for any acoustic, you will practice how to focus despite the sound you hear on the stage. Also, learn how to adjust quickly to the acoustic. If the stage is very dry, play slightly longer, giving short notes more ring, and take a bit quicker tempos when appropriate. However, in a very live space, you must adjust by playing even shorter and exaggerating articulation. Take slightly slower tempos, as fast things will just blur together in the hall.

SLEEP — We all know how stressful auditions can be. They often involve travel and sleeping in a strange environment. Quite a while ago, I was taking an important audition for a major orchestra. The audition was on a Monday morning, and my current orchestra had a 3pm Sunday concert. I had quite a long distance to travel by car, so I set off after that concert for the audition city. After a very long drive I arrived at a cute little B&B that I'd booked close to the hall. After settling in and reading a bit from my "quote journal," I laid down to go to sleep. I tossed and turned for several hours, not being able to fall asleep. Oh dear, it was 3am! I tried again. After several more tosses and turns, I looked at the clock. It was 5am, and still NO SLEEP! Once more I tried every trick in the book I knew for falling asleep. More tossing and turning. 7am, the alarm clock rings for my 10am audition time, and I've had NO SLEEP AT ALL!!

Now at this point, I know you are feeling a bit sorry for me, thinking, "there she goes again, another unsuccessful audition due to circumstance!" But no!! I got up, showered, went to the hall, played through 4 flawless rounds taking up the entire day and evening, winding up one of 2 finalists for this job! This was my secret – as part of my preparation, I actually PREPARED for no sleep! I know it sounds extreme, but I would actually stay awake the entire night, and then play several mock auditions the next day, observing how it felt at different times throughout the day, noting what my flaws were, where I needed to improve my focus and my strengths. I took this information and filed it away into my "audition bank." So when it actually happened for real, it did not scare or rattle me in the least. I knew how my body would react. I knew I would have the strength and focus to get successfully through many rounds of auditions. This knowledge saved me on that particular audition day!

I highly suggest that in Week 2 you incorporate as many *extremes* into your daily mocks as possible. Go the extra step! Be ready for anything... no, actually *prepare* for anything, and then enjoy the extra earned confidence that comes from having done this!

YOUR OUT OF TOWN MOCK AUDITION

If possible, try to get out of town this week for a formal mock. Bring along your journal, as the notes you obtain, and the observations you make during this trip, will be extremely useful come Audition Day. What did you eat? Where did you stay? How far in advance did you do your warm up? Was your outfit comfortable or distracting? Did your hair get in your face while playing? What shoes were you wearing? Everything you learn from this, both positive and negative, you will either recreate or discard for the actual Audition Day. Remember, we are talking about 6-10 total minutes! It's comparable to the "short program" in Olympic ice skating!! Do you think those skaters leave any tiny little detail to chance?

WEEK 2 SUMMARY

As Week 2 comes to a close you will have:

1) Solidified and played through your daily warm up for each day continuing through Audition Day
2) Followed your warm up with your (now very small) "naughty list"
3) Incorporated your "full potential self" exercise which takes place before each daily home mock audition
4) Recorded your daily mock auditions now with added intensity, listening back with a true sense of accomplishment and following up with your "nitty gritty" work
5) Prepared for extreme measures in your home mock auditions to the best of your ability
6) Continued reading your mental training books, jotting down quotes and now referring to those quotes as you go through your day
7) Incorporated several "virtual mocks" into your practice schedule
8) Traveled out of town if possible for a formal mock audition, keeping notes in your journal for future reference
9) Continued to take time to research your excerpts and play through FOR FUN now with a recording. This "virtual orchestra" in your head will be sure to join you at the audition!

6 WEEK COUNTDOWN!

	SUNDAY	MONDAY	TUESDAY	WEDNESDAY	THURSDAY	FRIDAY	SATURDAY
week 6	MARCH 27	28	29	30	31	APRIL 1	2
week 5	3	4	5	6	7	8	9
week 4	10	11	12	13	14	15	16
week 3	17	18	19	20	21	22	23
week 2	24	25	26	27	28	29	30
week 1	MAY 1	2	3	4	5	6	7
	8	AUDITION DAY!!! 9					

WEEK 1

Your audition is one week from today! I know you're feeling prepared, strong, and confident from all the hard work you have put in up to this point. In this last week it's important to tie up any loose ends you may have overlooked. Have you researched all your excerpts? Have you studied your mental training books? Are your journals well written in, with quotes and observations? Have you solidified your "useful" warm up? Is your "naughty list" almost if not completely empty? Are all of your travel arrangements set? Let's now enhance your positive self-talk.

"I LOVE THIS ONE!"

My practice/teaching studio is located pretty much in the center of the main floor of my house. Needless to say, both of my children can sing effortlessly and accurately any and every flute audition excerpt. Their renditions, complete with choreography at times, are highly amusing and entertaining. They also recently pointed out to me that before playing each excerpt I say "Oh, I love this one!" "Oh Mom, you say that about every excerpt!"

It's true, those words actually audibly come out of my mouth. And what's even more interesting is that *I actually DO love each and every one of them*! Really understanding the excerpts, coupled with working hard enough to play them well, honestly gives me great enjoyment. And I always hear the "virtual orchestra" in my head playing along, which makes them so much more meaningful and enjoyable. I've been able to carry this feeling to Audition Day, and really enjoy my time on stage. It is my hope that you'll also get to the point where every page you turn at the audition reveals another excerpt that elicits the "I love this one!" reaction. When this kicks in, you'll have a great time at the audition! And even if you don't experience that enthusiasm, try *saying* "I love this one!" before every excerpt you play this week. The power of suggestion can be very strong!

ENJOYMENT

I strongly believe that enjoyment is a key element in your preparation one week away from Audition Day. Be sure to spend a few minutes each day to just *enjoy* playing the flute! Play through sonatas, grab a colleague and play duets, put on some YouTube videos and play along. If you feel joy when you are playing your instrument, this will definitely transfer to the audition stage when you play your excerpts. It is so easy and common this close to audition day to associate anxiety with your instrument, which is why enjoyment is *so* important.

Enjoyment of life is also important in this week. Get a massage, take a yoga class, go to a spa. Treat yourself and your body well in this last week so you can also carry this relaxed and healthy feeling into the audition. There is nothing to be gained by becoming more and more stressed this last week. *Trust* your work and *trust* your preparation up to this point and add in some enjoyment!

GETTING NERVOUS IS NORMAL

At this point you have completed many mock auditions, some for your audio recorder, and hopefully some for a small committee. You've been using all the tools you've learned from your mental training studies. Yet, there is a chance that you still are getting nervous when put under pressure of playing excerpts for others. *This is normal! Don't worry!*

I learned many things from Billie Jean King's book "Pressure Is A Privilege," mostly that I could use a pressure situation, such as an audition, to my favor! No longer was it something to be feared, but rather something both stimulating and exciting. Pressure became my ally. It is important to note, however, that pressure and stress are very different from each other.

Stress often occurs when you haven't prepared properly. At this point in the 6-week regimen if you have followed the steps, you *have* prepared properly. You have kicked preparation's butt! You have earned permission to take doubt out of the equation, and believe in your discipline! What you will be feeling is pressure, not stress. Don't pretend that pressure doesn't exist, because it absolutely does. Talk about it, embrace it, make it work *for* you rather than against you!

I overheard a friend talking about the feeling in the warm up room just before the Personnel Manager knocked on his door to take him onstage for his audition round. He said he was so ready, so prepared he was almost shaking with excitement! He felt like a boxer just dying to enter the ring! His intense preparation allowed him to use this pressure situation to his advantage. Not surprising that this candidate went on to the final round of this very audition!

INDERAL STRAIGHT TALK

I recently taught a master class of varied levels and ages where we discussed performance anxiety for auditions and recitals, and I was literally shocked to hear that not one person in that room had even heard of Inderal! I feel it's definitely worth some mention, as I personally always use a small dosage for orchestral auditions. Inderal by definition is medication commonly prescribed to treat high blood pressure; it is a beta-adrenergic blocker that can also be used to treat irregular heartbeat, heart attack, migraine, and tremors. Propranolol is the generic equivalent. The key word here is "medication," which means that it is obtained by prescription only, and no one should try using this without first checking with your doctor!

It is helpful to first identify the physical symptoms you encounter when auditioning or performing. Does your heart race? Do you get dry mouth? Do your knees and/or hands shake? Do you become completely unfocused? Once you identify your physical nervous symptoms, know that Inderal is a beta blocker, which restricts the flow of adrenaline to your heart. If your heart races when you are nervous or overly excited, as mine does, then a small dosage of a beta blocker could prove to be very helpful for your performance. If your knees/hands shake, this medication will not be of any help. If you get dry mouth, Inderal will only exacerbate this symptom, as one of its side effects can be to cause even *more* dry mouth! There are many professionals who do not recommend taking beta blockers for performances, as blocking that adrenaline rush could actually dull your performance. It is undoubtably better to learn to *use* this adrenaline rush to our advantage for the best possible outcome, but for some, this just is not always possible by audition time, and I feel there is nothing worse than a heart that is racing out of control while you are trying to play a wind instrument! I would have to estimate by experience that there are probably just as many professional musicians taking Inderal occasionally as those who are not.

Your doctor will help you decide if this option is right for you and will prescribe the correct dosage. The many musicians I know who use this beta-blocker restrict the dosage to only 10 or 20 milligrams. It is also important to know that Inderal should be taken about two hours prior to audition time, so plan ahead. And probably the most important advice is that you *must* experiment with using Inderal several times before audition day! If you are thinking this may be a good option for you and you are new to this, try it in all of your formal mocks to evaluate what side effects you may have and how it will affect your performance!

YOUR COMPLETE MOCK

Near the beginning of Week 1, have a home mock audition where you play through your *entire* audition booklet, beginning to end, for your recorder. You may never have the time to listen back to all of it, but you *must* do this once. No stops, no distractions. Stay focused and just keep playing through, page by page. I remember doing this with one audition list and it took over an hour! However, at that particular audition, when I got to the Finals, the round consisted of about 80% of the entire list played onstage with no stops! I played for about 40 minutes straight, page by page, with the committee sitting there completely silent. I was very happy that my preparation included something so very similar to this, and I recall that another finalist could have been taken aback and distracted by that round being so very long and intense. Another huge benefit is that you can make a mental note of exactly what is not yet ready for this audition, including tutti sections that may have been neglected. You'll want to conserve your time and energy this week by practicing only what you *can't* play at this point!

After this mock has been completed, resume your regular routine by dividing up your cards into 2 or 3 rounds, and recording your home mocks followed by your nitty gritty practice. During this week, play one more formal mock audition, again keeping notes in your journal after you play and receive comments. Be sure to bring your extra audition booklet(s) to all formal mocks so the people listening to you can give you very specific comments. Try to arrange your mocks (both formal and home) around the time(s) of day that you most likely will be playing. Solidify your regimen so it becomes your routine, from eating to warm-up to focus exercises to excerpts, and use it each and every time. Also, it is extremely useful to do many "virtual" mock auditions in this week. The more successes you have, the more confident you will be when you hit that stage, and in a virtual mock, you play a great audition every time. Remember these take less than 10 minutes and produce amazing results!

WEEK 1 SUMMARY

As Week 1 comes to a close you will have:
1) Played through your entire audition booklet as a home mock for your recording device with no stops and no distractions
2) Solidified your Audition Day routine, beginning with your warm-up
3) Finished up all work on your "naughty list" and your "nitty gritty" practicing
4) Played many mock auditions including one formal, using as much variety as possible in locations and times of the day/evening
5) Continued with your mental training, reviewing all of your quotes and notes and trying some "full potential self" exercises
6) Learned to love and enjoy playing the flute, playing each excerpt, and spent some time relaxing and taking care of yourself including getting some extra rest
7) Included a few "virtual mock" auditions to your training, where you visualize a flawless and enjoyable audition every time
8) Commended and congratulated yourself for six weeks of intense training, feeling the strength, power, and confidence you now have earned

AUDITION DAY!

> "There is no stronger steel than well-founded belief in yourself; the knowledge that your preparation is fully complete and that you are ready for the competition. Confidence cannot be grafted on artificially. True abiding confidence is earned through tenaciously pursuing and attaining those assets that allow you to reach your own level of competency; that is, excellence."
>
> — John Wooden, from "The Pyramid of Success"[5]

From the moment you wake up until the moment you walk out of the audition venue for the last time, know that this day will be memorable. You will have visualized it in vivid detail countless times, so everything about this day will already feel familiar to you. From your exemplary preparation, you will feel positive, energized, and focused throughout the experiences of this day. Your heart is ready to engage in the musical experience of playing such great music. You will just be repeating for the umpteenth time the "enjoyable audition" you have already mocked in your practice. Your preparation is complete. It's time to let go and play. This is something you *get* to do, not *have* to do. Just as in a sports game, you *want* to be given the ball! After all, if you don't have the ball, you can't score. You're ready. You want to play your game. Take the ball! You've *chosen* to be here.

WHAT TO BRING

Pack carefully when you leave for the hall, as there may not be a chance to return to your hotel during an Audition Day. Besides the obvious (your instrument in great working condition), I suggest you bring:

1) Your audition excerpt packet
2) A water bottle
3) Snacks (all have of which been tried out in previous mock auditions!)
4) Your quote journal
5) Your audition journal (it is *very* helpful to write notes immediately following each audition round! I'll share a few of mine in the following pages.)
6) A sweater. I don't know what it is about the temperature in concert halls, but I've been freezing more often than not!
7) A book, magazine, and video-playing device to play your favorite video or even tv show. Sometimes there is a very long time between rounds if you advance, and leaving the Hall may not be a viable option. Bring something to keep you focused, entertained and calm. What would you bring if you had say a 3-hour plane ride?
8) A portable audio player and headphones! One of the hardest parts for me on Audition Day is the "waiting game." That is the seemingly endless amount of time from when you leave the stage until the Personnel Manager announces the committee's decision for your "round." This wait is often in a "group" room, so if you'd rather not hear about the other candidates' triumphs and woes, who is subbing with whom, who has just won this or that honor, you can happily revert to your own world with these two priceless items!

WHAT TO WEAR

I've seen literally every type of outfit at orchestral auditions, from ball gowns and tuxedos to sweats and a t-shirt! Most orchestras now have preliminary and semi-final rounds behind a screen, and you will have already done your homework to know this information for the orchestra you're auditioning for. If you are *only* playing a screened round on Audition Day, I suggest you dress as comfortably as possible, like you might for an orchestra rehearsal. The Committee will never see you, but the Personnel Manager will, and if you've done your preparation correctly, you'll be seeing this person for quite some time to come. Dress accordingly! If you are playing multiple rounds that day and might get to the final round (well, actually you *will* if you have followed all of the steps in this book!), be sure you're dressed appropriately for that. Many committee members may possibly be "old school," so a t-shirt and jeans will just *not* make a good impression. An orchestra audition is not, however, a concerto performance, so best to leave the extremely fancy duds behind.

Be comfortable, be classy!

YOUR MUSIC OR THEIRS?

This is an interesting and debatable question. More than likely, when you check in you'll be given a list of the music the Committee has chosen for the upcoming round. When it's getting closer to your audition time, you'll most likely be given a private warm up room containing a packet of the music you'll play on stage in the order provided. Many people, including me, prefer to play from their own parts, having simulated that in most if not every mock audition. However, you *must* carefully go through the Committee's packet excerpt by excerpt, carefully marking you own part with their start and stop place, any penciled-in dynamics, and eagle-eyeing any differences between their part and yours. (articulations? dynamics?) You must also be sure that your excerpts are prepared in the exact same order as their packet! Know that each member of the Committee will be looking at *their* packet, and you must not play something different, even if it's in your own part! To avoid all of this, you may just want to play from the packet given to you in the warm up room, which is perfectly fine.

YOUR PRIVATE WARM-UP TIME

The time always varies once you have a private warm up room, and having already solidified a routine for this all-important time is crucial! Every single person is different, and I cannot guess what would be the best routine for you. But you'll already have this information from your mock audition rounds.

Here are some things I've learned through experience:

1) Everyone else sounds AMAZING from their room! Don't listen! It's ultimately not the true case! My favorite coach John Wooden reminds us,

> "Respect your opponents but never fear them. You have nothing to fear if you have prepared to the best of your ability."[6]

2) Frantically playing through the list at top speed and volume does NOT usually

help you in those few minutes before walking onstage. My goodness, what if you suddenly make a mistake in *Classical Symphony*? *Voliere*? After playing it perfectly for weeks now, this one mistake will rattle you to your core and shake the focus right out of you!

3) Put your phone away. This is a time for extreme focus. Incorporating your "full potential self" exercises will benefit you infinitely more than checking in on Facebook!

4) Something you *will* have time for that will be very beneficial is to have one "virtual mock" in this warm up room, using the exact material you'll be playing in a few minutes on the stage. Breathe deeply and visualize yourself onstage playing each excerpt one by one, hearing the most beautiful sound and music coming from your flute and resonating throughout the hall, feeling yourself full of confidence and enjoyment. There is no possibility of mistakes with this kind of warm up, only a recipe for success!

YOUR MENTAL GAME

All of your hard work and practice leading up to this day will ensure that your fingers are ready to cooperate. All of your mental training leading up to this day will ensure that your brain will also cooperate! *These are equally important.* Whether you get nervous or not, your mental preparation will have given you the tools to use this to your advantage rather than disadvantage. I know I said it earlier, but it is worth repeating that it is *this* part of the triathlon I find least explored and most neglected by most candidates.

This unfortunately becomes apparent for many on audition day, as many a fine and accomplished player could not audition at the level they were capable of when their nerves worked against them. When interviewing my own Personnel Managers for this book, I asked what is the biggest mistake candidates seem to make at the audition. The answer was that it was not actually a "mistake," but the most common downfall was the candidate letting their nerves get the better of them, and having a lack of *mental* preparation and focus.

I read a heartbreaking yet very well written article by a musician who put his entire life on hold and worked diligently, practicing upwards of eight hours a day for many months, for a particular audition that held great importance to him. In his mind, he left no stone unturned, pushing himself to his physical limit in preparation. It was difficult to read his tale of Audition Day, knowing the amount of hours and sweat he had put into preparing. However, at the audition he became unfocused and distracted for a split second, and then became completely derailed. I felt for this man, yet noticed that he had a huge hole in his preparation. All those hours in the practice room, but virtually no hours spent on his mental preparation, was the one thing that failed him in the end! Most people get nervous. I always get nervous. *Prepare yourself for this and do your mental training!*

SHOULD I PLAY SOME "TEST" NOTES ON THE STAGE?

I often get asked whether or not to play a few notes when you get onto the stage before starting the first required excerpt. There is not a clear yes or no answer to this, however, the following advice may be helpful. You must keep in mind two very important things:

1) If you choose to play a few notes, these are the very first notes the committee will hear from you. They must be the most beautiful, perfectly in tune, clearly articulated, and filled-with-intent notes you have ever played! First impressions are formed with first sounds from behind that screen, and we all know there are no second chances at first impressions. If you feel it's important to "test" notes on the stage, please keep this in mind!

2) Much of this preparation method you've been following has been based on routine. If you want to play "test" notes on the stage, I urge you to include that in your mock auditions leading up to this day, as well as your "virtual" mocks. You have played out this scene many times before the actual audition, so be sure you have included *this* aspect as well.

THE WAITING GAME

I find few things in life more uncomfortable or even more intimidating than a green room of flute colleagues waiting on the arrival of the Personnel Manager to announce if you will or will not advance. This has to be my very least favorite part of taking an audition. I find it comforting to have my headphones on and a book in hand to keep me company for this seemingly endless wait. I personally do not want to chat at auditions. It is easily distracting, but more importantly my preparation routine did not include chatting at any point. I want to "stick to the script" as best I can to remain focused throughout the rounds.

This was particularly hard at one audition I took, as a very close friend whom I hadn't seen in many years (because she was playing in an orchestra out of the country) was in my round. I did make the difficult choice to keep to myself, and was able to remain focused and on task for the rest of this successful audition. But unfortunately, I never got the chance to catch up with my friend! If by chance you are not passed on to the next round, ask yourself if you believe that you did your best. A very wise man (John Wooden) said,

> "I believe there is nothing wrong with the other fellow being better than you if you are prepared and are functioning in the way you've tried to prepare. That's all you can do. You never fail if you know in your heart that you did the best of which you are capable."[7]

PERFORMANCE VS. OUTCOME GOALS

I learned and began implementing a very important lesson after studying James Loehr's book, "The Mental Game." Confidence is directly tied to perceived success. Therefore, the goals you set for your audition time (and also for all of the mocks you have been doing to this point) must be attainable. If you set goals that are beyond your control, you will likely lose control of your confidence. Therefore, it's important to set Performance goals, rather than Outcome goals.

Examples of PERFORMANCE goals may be:
1) I will give 100% to this audition.
2) I will have a great attitude from the moment I walk on the stage until the moment I leave the stage.
3) I will play each excerpt as musically as possible.
4) I will play with as much contrast as I possibly can.
5) I will monitor my breathing throughout the audition, making sure to take relaxed breaths.
6) I will envision the committee smiling throughout my audition.
7) I will do the very best I can.
8) I accept whatever comes out in this audition.

Examples of OUTCOME goals that you need to avoid while on the stage are:
1) I have to pass into the next round of the audition.
2) I will impress this committee.
3) I will play every excerpt perfectly.

I added #8 to my list of Performance Goals after reading Kenny Werner's incredibly enlightening book "Effortless Mastery." He opened my eyes to many wonderful ideas, one of them being to STOP TRYING TO SOUND GOOD. You are already good! You are already prepared! It's when we stop trying so hard that we are able to let go and just play! Therefore, his words made a huge impact on my thinking, thus adding to my Performance Goal list.

> "I accept whatever comes out. I accept it with love. Without the drama of needing to sound good. I play from an effortless space."[8]

Aaron Goldman, Principal Flutist of the National Symphony said when interviewed by *Flute Talk* magazine about his audition for that position,

> "I decided to take the audition with the goal of performing well for my colleagues, not necessarily winning the job. In the end, I think this mindset helped me in the audition. It freed me from any expectations."[9]

Each person will be able to come up with a slightly different set of Performance goals most useful to them. Be sure, though, to set realistic rather than unrealistic goals. Don't confuse who you really are with whom you wish to be. Unrealistic goals eventually lead to shattered confidence, and confidence is the name of the game for your time onstage!

THOUGHTS FROM A PERSONNEL MANAGER'S POINT OF VIEW

The Personnel Manager sees it all! Beginning with the initial letter or résumé you send, and ending with the very final moments on Audition Day, they are the one person who has interacted with literally hundreds, even thousands of audition candidates, hearing every round from the best seat in the house, onstage next to the candidate. I had the great opportunity to interview two of our own Detroit Symphony Personnel Managers and would like to pass on their invaluable insight to you.

SS: What do you feel is the biggest mistake audition candidates make on audition day?
PM1: People come unprepared thinking something that hasn't been working in the practice room will somehow magically work for them onstage. Inevitably, there is a huge amount of lack of preparation in many candidates that come to our auditions. The level of preparation and accuracy has to be SO high before setting foot on the stage. You have to be ready to play.
PM2: Not taking mental preparation seriously enough. I've seen many great players seem to let their nerves get the better of them onstage.

SS: When playing a round onstage at an audition, what is the most common thing candidates do to lessen their chances of advancement?
PM1: I see too many candidates race through the list, not taking any time to breathe in between excerpts. They do not take the time to mentally set the next excerpt up before beginning.
PM2: I am personally shocked at the number of candidates who do not count the rests in the music correctly or carefully! Rests matter as much as the notes, and the comittee members notice when the rests aren't correct.

SS: What is the most helpful hint you have for a candidate during the audition round?
PM1: Pay attention to details! Every detail, no matter how small is extremely important, including note lengths, dynamics, accents, etc. Also, pay great attention throughout the entire audition to the quality of sound. Too many players lose focus of the sound and also tend to push the sound past the point of excellent quality. This happens on ALL instruments, strings and winds alike.
PM2: Hands down, preparation and attention to detail!

SS: What have you observed in backstage behavior that can either help or hurt a candidate?
PM1: Some auditionees fall into a "schmooze" mode at the audition. They see their friends and treat it more like a night out on the town rather than an audition. I've seen many of these candidates lose their focus and diminish their chances of advancing when falling prey to the socializing temptations at the audition.

PM2: Trying to gather too much information, such as who else is at or coming to the audition. How many have advanced already? How many and who was asked to the invited rounds? Not only is this *not* OK to ask, as it will put the Personnel Manager in an awkward position, but I've also seen it totally derail and distract the candidate from the task at hand once they actually found out the information, either from the Personnel Manager or another candidate at the audition.

SS: You have both been onstage for many, many auditions. What do you feel is ok for the candidate to ask you while onstage during a round?

PM1: It is always ok to ask me to ask the committee's permission if you would like to repeat a botched excerpt. This is especially ok if it has been a long audition round. However, I would not advise doing this a repeated number of times in any given round.

PM2: Please feel free to ask us if something in the music or part is unclear, such as repeats, articulation, etc. It is much better to clarify this with us then to be left wondering after you have begun to play.

SS: After hearing many auditions, can you offer any other useful advice to auditionees?

PM1: Yes! Here are 4 important things:

1) When you are playing solo material, you must prepare to capture the listener.
2) Don't treat the screen as a buffer. Play each round as if there is no screen and you are truly representing yourself, not hiding your identity.
3) We WANT people to do their very best because we WANT to hire someone!
4) If you don't have the time to really prepare, and I mean thoroughly and completely, stay home.

PM2: These sound like common sense, but I've seen too many people who did not know these things:

1) If your audition time slot is between 11 and 12, do not arrive at the hall at 11am! You may have to play at 11:05!
2) Dress comfortably for screened rounds. I'm not sure why men show up in complete formal suit and tie for a screened round, or women in very high heeled shoes, unless that is the outfit they actually do play most comfortably in!
3) Please read all information we send you carefully and meticulously. I have had to answer SO many questions on and before Audition Day that I had already included in material sent to each candidate!
4) As PM1 said, we WANT to hire someone, probably more than anyone else associated with the audition!

TO REST OR NOT TO REST…

The Personnel Managers alluded to this, but I must take a moment to emphasize it…YES! Count the rests! And count them carefully and accurately. I'm not talking about LONG periods of rests where you would not play (for example the 13 measures after the beginning of Leonore), but ANY and all short rests MUST be counted and left in. (For example in the Mozart *Concerto in G* exposition; the 5 measures rest following the opening 4 bars of Mendelssohn's *Scherzo* before the long solo; the measures in between the opening measures of *Daphnis)*. And here's where your "Virtual Orchestra" can help you immensely. You will be hearing them in your head, so all of your entrances will be placed perfectly as if you were sitting in the orchestra. Trust me when I say that your Committee has brought this Virtual Orchestra to the audition as well, and you have a much better chance of staying in sync with them throughout your audition if you include (silent) orchestral music in your rests!

PLAY IT AGAIN, SAM…

Often I have been asked whether it's acceptable to a committee if the candidate asks the Personnel Manager to ask the committee if they can repeat a botched excerpt during the audition. This is absolutely a case-by-case basis, however, based on my experience from being on the committee: only ask if the excerpt was played poorly after your other excerpts all went well, and *only* if you're positive it will go well on the second try. It will hurt your chances if you ask and then can't execute it perfectly on second try! Also, it's like a "get out of jail free" card, so use it sparingly. Only ask once if at all. I personally have not been on a committee that has ever denied a candidate a second try when they asked for it. But I have seen it happen many times that a candidate asks to repeat, then cannot execute any better the second time, hence hurting their chances.

It is quite common especially in the semi-final or final round that the committee will ask the candidate to play an excerpt again, hopefully accompanied by a certain directive, such as play it softer, louder, keeping better tempo, paying strict attention to rhythm, etc. It's to your advantage to listen very carefully to this directive, and to really exaggerate what they want to hear from you! If they have asked you, they want it to be different, and also, they like you.

In one audition semi-final round I played in, the committee asked me to play an excerpt softer. 3 excerpts later, they asked for another excerpt softer, and even once again two excerpts after that, "please play again and softer!" By that point, (although I should have caught on to this much sooner) it occurred to me that it must sound much louder out in the hall than onstage, as I was already playing what I felt was super soft. By the third excerpt of this request, I took a chance and played the excerpt so it was barely even audible to me onstage. They loved it! I believe that alone got me advanced to the finals that day!

And speaking of soft playing, I really want to share this next piece of advice with you. It's something I've seen time and time again, audition after audition, but only remembered to add to this book while watching the Super Bowl this past year. I was texting with my son, who is extremely knowledgeable of all things sports. Many people were kind of stunned that the Broncos were winning against the favored Panthers and their superstar quarterback, Cam Newton. My son understood and said, "Defense wins championships." Suddenly I thought about auditions, and realized it's not flashy, technical, superstar playing that wins auditions, however in my experience "Soft playing wins auditions." There is nothing as impressive as a player who can play super soft, controlled, in tune, and musically in an audition. Loud playing happens all day long, but it's true, just as "defense wins championships" in football, "soft playing wins auditions."

AUXILIARY INSTRUMENTS

Many auditions require you to play and bring more than one instrument onstage with you. Please plan ahead for this, as you'll want to have a convenient place to set these instruments as well as the proper swabs, etc., for them. Be sure in your preparation you have prepared to switch from one instrument to the next with ease, and this does not throw you at the audition. If a very small number of excerpts are on the list for the auxiliary instrument (such as piccolo for a 2nd Flute audition) you must be very sure you sound equally prepared and amazing on that instrument as well! I personally know of a story where when down to two finalists for a 2nd Flute position, one candidate edged above the other due in large part to her finesse on the piccolo!

You may wonder if it is acceptable to play a few trial notes on a new instrument you must switch to during an audition round. I have found that this is acceptable (and even advised), EXCEPT in the case of playing an excerpt that requires you switch instruments DURING the excerpt (such as the *New World Symphony* or the end of *Daphnis*). The committee will want to know you can make this switch while counting rests correctly and coming in perfectly on your new instrument without "testing" any notes first, just as you would have to do in that piece in the orchestra.

A SNEAK PEEK THROUGH TO THE OTHER SIDE OF THE SCREEN

You are candidate #53. We (the committee) are on Day 3 and have only passed two people onto the semi-final round. We are attentive yet tired, restless, hungry, distracted. We're hoping the lunch menu is better than the day before, that they can somehow turn the darned air-conditioning down in the hall, but mostly that you, candidate #53 will *come out and play your a%#@ off!* That's right, we're not hoping you'll mess up that run in *Classical Symphony*, that your descending scale in *Leonore* will go flat, WE WANT YOU TO NAIL IT!!! We want your concerto excerpt, often the first thing we'll hear, to be beautiful, musical, magical, or at the very least beautiful, in tune, and in rhythm! We want to advance you! We want to love you! You start with a full deck of cards, so all you need to do is *give us what we want!*

I have a very good friend who always says to anyone before an audition, "Go out there and show them what you *can* do, not what you *can't!*" So when you are playing your audition, imagine a group of individuals behind that screen who already love you before you even play a note. They are your biggest fans. It's simple and true, we don't want to judge you, *we want to enjoy you!*

photo credit: Randall Hawes

ACTUAL NOTES FROM MY LITTLE NOTEPAD

I recently reviewed my notes from the last audition committee I sat on, which happened to be a flute audition. I was really struck by the number of times I wrote the same comments over and over, from candidate to candidate. I decided to start counting up some of them just to see exactly how many times I repeated the following comments, and formulated this "Top 8" list. These are the top 8 comments, in descending order, that resulted in candidates not advancing at this audition. Once tabulated, it was pretty eye opening! These comments were taken from the 79 preliminary auditions that I heard:

8) very loud breathing (24 times)
7) not completely clean (32 times)
   (Most players believe that if they don't play completely cleanly they will be eliminated. However, I found that more often than not, a committee collectively would still want to pass those players to the next round if a very small imperfection of technique was their only audition round flaw.)
6) articulation not clear (34 times, especially low notes!)
5) needs more diminuendo (41 times, most memorably *Leonore* opening measures, right out of the gate!)
4) count rests more carefully (47 times, including late after the breath!)
3) needs more dynamic contrast (49 times)
2) rhythm not steady (55 times)

… and the number one comment that eliminated players from this Preliminary round… *(drum roll, please)*

1) INTONATION ISSUES (105 times!)

Please take note of a couple of things here:

Not completely clean will most likely *not* eliminate you from a preliminary round. If you make a small blip and immediately recover, you are still on track to possible advancement. Try not to let a small blip make you lose your focus!

Great intonation is crucial!! The entire committee will be unforgiving to a candidate who has intonation issues. And the way you prepare can simply eliminate intonation issues! The committee begs you to play in tune! And the nitty gritty way you've prepared can simply help you to eliminate those intonation issues that are so crucial to a successful audition. With 79 candidates, there were 105 instances of poor intonation!

Contrast matters! Detroit's Orchestra Hall is a great yet challenging venue to show true contrast of dynamics. The entire committee was desperate for a candidate who could play the opening G of the Beethoven *Leonore* excerpt at a true *ff* (yet in tune!) and diminuendo to a true *p*, hold the scale there (again, in tune!) and play the ensuing triplets at the marked *pp*. You'd be extremely surprised how rare this is, and how appreciated it is when executed.

I often joke with my students about this imaginary box they are all standing in for most of their lessons and performances. I call it "the mezzo box." Everything sounds *mp* or *mf* to the listener! They are so afraid to come OUT of that box! Sometimes I make them physically jump out of an imaginary box to either side of it and exclaim, "There, now you are out! Play forte! Or jump to the other side…. You are out! Play piano!" I cannot begin to tell you how many audition candidates in a row will play inside that box. For your time on stage, please step out of the mezzo box!

THE DEVIL IS IN THE DETAILS! As our Personnel Managers pointed out earlier, attention to detail is extremely important in an audition. Not only must you pay attention to every printed detail on the page of the excerpt, but also the all-important small details of note beginnings, endings, breath length, exact rhythms, articulations, dynamics, etc.

VI. "Der Abschied" from Das Lied von der Erde by Gustav Mahler, ed. Jeanne Baxtresser ORCHESTRAL EXCERPTS FOR FLUTE, © 1995 by Theodore Presser Company, Used by permission.

THE AFTERMATH: LIFE AFTER AUDITION DAY

An audition is an *event*. It takes intense training, time, discipline, determination, and focus. And like any event, once it is completed you'll need time to reflect and recover, no matter what the outcome. If you have trained properly, I guarantee you'll feel the immense strength and progress you have not only gained. but in fact, earned. This may not be an immediate feeling, but it will undoubtably happen.

ASK AND YOU SHALL RECEIVE

Once the audition is over, it is very important to collect and review any and all data that you can. Hopefully you kept notes in your Audition Journal on the day of the audition. These notes will serve you well on your next audition, even if a long time passes in between. It is also very helpful to compare *your* notes to the notes of the audition committee, which brings me to this suggestion: ASK FOR COMMENTS!

I know that some orchestras discourage this, and even include it in the written materials they send to you. However, it certainly does not hurt to ask regardless, as this information can prove to be of great value to you. I have never refused to give comments for any request I have ever received, either directly from a candidate or from our Personnel office.

The best way to go about this is *not* on audition day, but very shortly after by sending a very professional and cordial email to the personnel manager. This email must include your audition number! I received a request for comments once stating, "I was in the morning group on Monday." This is not helpful, as we need your exact audition number to provide you with comments. Also, the sooner you do this after the audition the better, as many committee members do not hang onto these comments very long after the audition is over.

Once you've collected comments, review them intelligently, knowing that they can often be confusing and conflicting. One committee member could say "articulation too short" while another says "articulation too long" for the same excerpt! As you gain experience, you will learn which comments are truly most helpful and useful for you.

I really have to insert a very funny story here as I recently found my "audition journal" notes from a semi-final round of an audition that I took many years ago. These notes were from the semi-final round and written by me in my Audition Journal immediately following leaving the stage:

Mozart: high D sounds airy and out of tune. Had a little more life though, and no cracked notes!

Leonore: went much better, felt much freer.

Brahms 4: I think I was out of tune and probably too loud. They didn't say anything, though.

Peter and the Wolf: thought it was fine. Had fun! Heard the other semi-finalist play this in the warm up room at break neck speed and totally clean! Arrgh!

Brahms 2: Really put my ALL into it! They responded, "You don't have to carry the WHOLE ORCHESTRA there! Please play less loud, more accurate and make more of the accent." Played it again…softer…I think??

Mendelssohn 4: Tried to play SUPER SOFT to show I could do it. I think it worked well!

Classical Symphony 2nd movement: Also tried VERY SOFT. Kept my tempo and high A spoke really nicely.
4th movement: All worked OK; high D's were pretty sharp. That was all probably TOO LOUD, too!

Daphnis: opening went well. Tried to count rests really carefully this time. No comment from Committee. Page 4 (after flute solo): SUCKED ONCE AGAIN. THE SPEW EXCERPT!! NEED TO NAIL THIS if I EVER take a 2nd flute audition ever again!! They skipped over next 2 excerpts.

Bartók: went fine, no cracks. I tried again not to play so loudly. No comments. Maybe they are getting bored of me. Needed to step it up!

Skipped Britten excerpt (good!) and Scherzo.

Piccolo solo: (Vivaldi concerto 2nd movement) I think it really sucked but it could have been even worse. I need to buy my own piccolo! (I borrowed one for the audition!). Can't believe they wanted to hear Dvořák after that! Went ok but sounded out of tune to me.

Dvořák Flute solos: ok, probably TOO LOUD!

That was it… they said "Thank you, nice audition." Yeah yeah, as in "Have a nice life!" All in all not too bad. Lesson Learned for the next time for sure! Was not nervous, rather excited! But need to be a little more relaxed and focused in the future.

The really funny part of this is that I actually WON this audition! And after winning and joining this orchestra, I have heard for years from the people on that very same committee that this particular semi-final round was in their words "one of the best auditions they had ever heard! It was a perfect audition in every way!" Go figure!

You just never know what the committee is thinking, and you HAVE to stay in the moment, keeping your head in the game from first note until last, not judging your flaws! This was an amazing lesson for me, and I was really lucky to have first of all recorded my thoughts, and then heard the committee's perspective on that very same audition round. I hope you will learn from this story as well!

SUCCESS

The fact is, out of everyone who participates in any audition, there can only be the possibility of one person ultimately being offered the position. That means that everyone else at the audition will *not* be offered the position. But please do not confuse this with "winning." We all have our own definition of what winning or success means. I believe the real accomplishment lies in the journey, rather than the outcome. Let a successful journey become your destination. However, you can't fool yourself. When the outcome is announced, only *you* will know in your heart if you have truly put in every effort that you were capable of. If that's the case, you *will* truly feel successful, regardless of the outcome.

My definition of "success" comes from Coach John Wooden, the famous former basketball coach from UCLA, referred to elsewhere in this book:

> "Success is giving 100% of your effort, body, mind, and soul to the struggle. True success is knowing you did everything within the limits of your ability to become the very best that you are capable of being. YOU are totally in control of your success!" [10]

Once I devised this 6-week system and began using it, I felt two really amazing things that I had never felt before at auditions. The first was the belief, *real* belief in my heart, that no one, not one person at that audition, could have out-prepared or worked any harder than I did. The second came after I played, that no matter what the committee said, I already felt like a winner for the immense progress I had made and for the invaluable tools I had accumulated on this journey to audition day. Nothing could ever take that away from me. My level had been raised, my game forever upped.

If you did not advance at this audition, it is only temporary, and not all-encompassing. Study the day, learn from it, and then have the self-control to forget about it. You need not look far in the world of sports to find examples to support this.

Tony Dungy, former coach of the Indianapolis Colts, puts this into perspective in his book "Uncommon."

> "I've learned that if you are afraid of failure, you won't try to do very much. But if you are going to chase meaningful dreams and do significant things, you have to be willing to come up short sometimes. I admire people for the way they handle failures. Success is really a journey of persistence and perseverance in spirit of failure." [11]

One of the best football quarterbacks of all time, Peyton Manning, had one of those "terrible, horrible, no good days," however his was in front of millions of people at the 2014 Super Bowl. *The Super Bowl, for goodness sakes!* Regardless of how hard he trained, prepared, conditioned, nothing went his way that day. Many would say that would be the end to his career. However, Peyton knew he had done his best. And he had the self-control to forget about it. He came back to win many other games, and two years after that horrible day, led his team to win Super Bowl 50!

He is a true champion. In one of the best sports speeches I have ever heard, Peyton spoke about talent vs. preparation. His words resonated so clearly with what I have always believed, "There were other players who were more talented, but there was no one who outprepared me. And for this reason, I have no regrets."

When unseeded women's tennis player Roberta Vinci defeated No. 1 seeded Serena Williams in the semi-finals of the 2015 US Open, Serena walked off the court waving one finger in the air at the crowd, as if to say, "I'm number one. I am a winner." As commentator Chris Evert put it, "The one thing you know about Serena is that no matter what she's feeling, or the state of her game, she will believe the title is hers for the taking."

She may have lost that one match, but she is still a winner, a true champion. Even if these champions were not always "offered the one position open," they were always successful and believed in their success. Hopefully you will walk away from your next audition feeling the same!

I have one final thought to leave you with. In the 25 years of my professional career, one thing is always true — there will always be another audition. And another and another. And just when you think there may not be, there will be yet another. It is my sincere hope that you will walk away from your next audition feeling successful, with whatever that definition now means to you, and you will have learned to enjoy this roller coaster of an endeavor, embracing the preparation and process more than the outcome. *Whether you realize or not, you have already won.*

ACKNOWLEDGMENTS

I have so much gratitude for my mentors, Julius Baker, Thomas Nyfenger, and Geoffrey Gilbert, who taught me all I know about the flute, and inspired me to be the best musician I could be.

Thank you to my closest "flute friends," Jeffery Zook, Linda Toote, and Robin Peery, who inspire me on a daily basis not only with their playing but with their unending lifelong friendship and support.

Thank you to Donna Orbovich who opened up a whole new world of discovering my "full potential self" and is my full-time support system and amazing friend.

A huge thank you to Jeffrey Barker, who helped me to remember my original plan week by week, tested out all of the methods, gave so generously of his time, and without whom I believe I never would have completed this book!

I am sincerely grateful to Daniel Dorff of Theodore Presser Company, who first believed in the concept of this book, then spent endless hours editing, researching, and perfecting each and every sentence with me, all the while inserting his immense knowledge, experience, and refreshing sense of humor.

And a huge thank you to Hannah and Zack, who are my inspiration, comic relief, and the most rewarding, patient, and special part of my life.

PERMISSIONS

1. Chris Evert, "Tennis" Magazine, September/October 2015 issue, page 4; Chrissie's View Column (Vol. 51, No. 5), Tennis Media Company, LLC, 48 West 21st Street; 6th Floor, New York, NY 10010.
2. Billie Jean King, "Pressure is a Privilege" published by Life Time Media, Inc., www.lifetimemedia.com.
3. Wooden: A Lifetime of Observations and Reflections On and Off the Court, John Wooden with Steve Jamison, McGraw-Hill, used by permission.
4. Billie Jean King, "Pressure is a Privilege" published by Life Time Media, Inc., www.lifetimemedia.com.
5. John Wooden, "The Pyramid of Success."
6. Wooden: A Lifetime of Observations and Reflections On and Off the Court.
7. Wooden: A Lifetime of Observations and Reflections On and Off the Court.
8. Kenny Werner, "Effortless Mastery" published by Jamey Abersold Jazz; PO Box 1244; New Albany, IN 47151; www.jazzbooks.com) page 117, awaiting permission.
9. Patricia George, "Thoughts on Auditioning from Aaron Goldman," Flute Talk, July/August 2013.
10. Wooden: A Lifetime of Observations and Reflections On and Off the Court.
11 Some content taken from 'UNCOMMON' by Tony Dungy. Copyright © 2009, 2011. Used by permission of Tyndale House Publishers, Inc. All rights reserved.